Amnesiac

Neil Jordan

Amnesiac

A Memoir

HEAD
ZEUS

An Apollo Book

First published in the UK in 2024 by Head of Zeus Ltd,
part of Bloomsbury Publishing Plc

9 7 5 3 1 2 4 6 8

A catalogue record for this book is available from the British Library.

ISBN (HB): 9781804549957
ISBN (XTPB): 9781035912971
ISBN (E): 9781804549933

Printed and bound in Great Britain by
CPI Group (UK) Ltd, Croydon CR0 4YY

Head of Zeus Ltd
First Floor East
5–8 Hardwick Street
London EC1R 4RG

WWW.HEADOFZEUS.COM

For Jenne Casarotto
Wish you were here

A Hole in the Heart

I was driving round the mouth of the Boyne with Angela, my mother, visiting the landscapes of her childhood, and the memories seemed to change with the weather. You know the kind of weather, where a blast of wind can turn a sunlit September afternoon into a downpour. Was it September? I'm not sure. It was the autumn of her life anyway. She was in her eighties and had discovered, about a decade ago, that she had that odd Edwardian or Victorian thing, 'a hole in the heart'. For a woman so active, with a heart so large, it was hard to picture it as a kind of *Titanic* pierced by an underwater needle of ice, or as a dirigible, one of those outlandish balloons gliding over the landscape of her memories with a hidden deflation in the stitching. What the doctors meant was not so much a hole as an inherited defect, an artificial enlargement of one side or the other. Anyway, she had entered the strange landscape of the sick soon after that news, which to me meant the dismal car park of Beaumont Hospital, listening to Bob Dylan on the car radio sing 'Not Dark Yet'. If it wasn't dark yet, it was getting there. As appropriate a soundtrack as any to the smoking area under the Perspex rain umbrella, next to the bus stop with a corrugated metal roof where you could have a rainless cigarette too but weren't meant to, on your way to the warren of Portakabins around the back near where the garbage was waiting for collection, inside of where I might find her on a trolley, in a corridor, waiting, like the garbage cans, for the attention of a professional. A doctor in her case.

The doctor, oddly enough, was a boy I had known, who lived in a grander house up the road, whose father in turn was a doctor, and whose grandmother used to sit in the upstairs bedroom window, immobile and outraged while we robbed the apples from their rather perfect fairy-tale orchard. She wasn't wearing a moth-eaten wedding dress, but something about her immobility and her silent fury always reminded me

Painting, Boyne Estuary, Angela Jordan.

of Miss Havisham. How did Dickens always manage to nail the archetype? What larks, Pip. No one else had an orchard as carefully tended as this, and nobody had such fairy-tale apples, quite so luscious and biblically red. We filled our tattered jumpers with the apples, and slid away like snakes through the long grass of the old seminary behind, Manresa House. The perfect crime, we imagined, although the problem then was what to do with the apples? You can only eat so many. The theft was the thing, the crime was perfect, only the old woman saw us. Let's dump them in the long grass and come back for them tomorrow.

Although I arrived home to discover there are no perfect crimes. My mother already knew. The doctor, son of the outraged Miss Havisham by the upstairs window and father of the doctor now treating her ailing heart, had come knocking on her door. It's about Neil. She almost had her first heart attack, imaging her son dead under the wheels of the 30 bus on the Clontarf Road, and he had to reassure her, no, it's nothing, just about some stolen apples.

Did he remember, this grandson of Miss Havisham? He looked so medicinal and authoritative in his white coat, with his stethoscope dangling, in this unlovely corridor of Portakabins where she was waiting on her very own metal trolley. But, no, he was kind. We were both far beyond stolen apples and perfect childhood crimes. He discussed her heart and the artificial device he had implanted next to it, how it would solve one problem but create another. How that other problem might eventually affect what he called her 'quality of life'. By which he meant, the more dependent she would be on it, the weaker she would get. I eased her into the wheelchair and offered to pay to move her to private facilities on the Southside, Vincent's or the Blackrock Clinic, but no, she said, she would have to get used to becoming like the Tin Man in *The Wizard of Oz* and wanted to be near the doctor she knew and the house we had grown up in.

So I had collected her from that house, looking out on St Anne's Estate and to remind her of happier times driven her past the airport towards Drogheda, a drive we used to take as kids every summer, to the small, ramshackle, sand-blown villages of Laytown and Bettystown. There was a meandering river called the Nanny, a ridiculous name even to a child, but then maybe that Nanny was no more ridiculous than that Betty and she had a whole village named after her. With a permanent carnival at the back of a pub with a thatched roof. Although to call it a carnival would be to lend it a grandeur it didn't deserve. A raised platform of metal with dodgem cars that trundled in meandering circles. I remember rolling underneath it with a skinny girl from the North of Ireland. She wanted to kiss me and I can still feel her protruding teeth, with bands of metal around them. Braces. Who wore braces then? Girls from Belfast, maybe. A few swings across from it, and some kind of up and down attempt at a roller coaster. A dark corrugated iron hall with slot machines. There had been a blacksmith's I remember, or think I remember, across the way, a stone cavern with, again, a corrugated metal roof. The smell of red-hot metal, a fire crackling towards the back, stories of a mythical character called the Bull Brennan who had fathered children with half the women of the hinterland. He came and went, apparently, with the harvests, doing seasonal work in the fields.

A triangle of concrete outside of the carnival which always had miniature sand dunes in the cracks, blown by the wind which came from the beach and sea, always visible behind the shop with the corrugated iron roof which played like an African drum when the rains came down, which was every day. What was the name? Plunkett's or Lydon's? No, it was something more to do with the seasons. Winter, Spring or Summer. Sommers, in fact. They couldn't have been called Winters. Then there wouldn't have been the sand, blowing in through the open door, the beach balls stacked in rows deep in the interior, and the squeals of delight from the carnival across the way and the girl with the dyed blonde hair who served behind the counter. Anyway, I drove my mother out that way to find the fields still unchanged, the bridge still visible above the river, with its tiny walkway tracking the railway above, from one side to the other, but everything else unrecognizable. It had become a suburb of Drogheda, complete with the unlovely sprawl of bungalows and a four-storey hotel-cum-apartment block. The single main street seemed to have attracted developments of quite ferocious ugliness the way her hospital in Beaumont collected plastic rubbish bins and Portakabins. So I kept driving, to a place called Mornington, perched above the Boyne river and we stopped at a small coffee shop, which used to be a post office, and ordered two coffees in the cramped interior and whether we had them there, on the white plastic chairs or on the green metallic garden chairs outside, I don't remember but I do remember her telling me: I was born here.

Memory

But then I don't trust memory. I was asked to write this memoir by a publisher – who remembered me. He had been a year behind me in the same school, or maybe two; he was in the same class as my brother. My brother was a diligent student, uncannily good at maths, as was my father. I was dreadful at maths but I had a particular talent for geometry. In fact I got close to 100 per cent on a geometry test, and close to zero on arithmetic, algebra, trigonometry and whatever other categories mathematics was divided into in those days. Probably because pictures made sense to me while numbers didn't. Pictures were my mother's world, numbers were my father's. The difference between the marks was so extreme that the teacher came to the conclusion that I had copied from someone else. As he prepared to administer the punishment – probably six on either hand – I had to point out one flaw in his deductive logic. That nobody else had attained the same result in geometry, so who could I possibly have copied from? That gave him some pause, but not much. And his response was, I had to admit to myself, rational, at least from his standpoint. But it taught me that rationality has its limits, that pictures are better than numbers because they don't always have to make sense. That the punishment rarely fits the crime and mathematics is useless as a description of an irrational world.

Maiden

I was born here.

Had she told me that before? She must have. But for some reason it hit home. Of course, I thought, that's why we spent so much time in the village nearby, in small cottages with rattling roofs of tin. That's why we came here every summer, to spend solid months of exquisite boredom among those dunes. That's why I wrote those stories, of sea, sand and discovery and disappointment. That's why her sister Ita retired to a tiny cottage on the Laytown Road while her husband Pearse built a boat in the back garden that could have sailed to the Azores but never left the cement blocks that sank ever deeper into the grass. That's why my father had asked, with some embarrassment, to borrow money so they could buy a mobile home in Lynch's Caravan Site and I had an odd, perverse delight in coming up with it, as if some paternal scales had been weighted in a new direction. That's why he was fishing in the Nanny river when he died, of a heart attack, and got my daughter safely to the shore before the inevitable happened. That's why I used the same estuary with the bridge above it in my first movie, *Angel*, and returned to it anytime I needed a location or an image that struck an emotional chord. I had to situate a carnival for the opening of *The Crying Game* and placed it on the spit of land, still visible beneath the pillars of the railway bridge, with the river curving round the edges of the tents. I could even use the walkway beneath it for the camera tracks. And at a loss for a location for a surreptitious conversation between Michael Collins and the Castle spy Ned Broy, I placed them on the same walkway, with the Dublin to Drogheda train trundling overhead. That's why I saw that kingfisher dart among the rushes, while staring at what I thought was an enormous dead flatfish just below the muddy bank. Maybe even why I didn't spear it with the bamboo stick until it flashed away up the river, faster even than the kingfisher. That's why I've always felt at home in estuaries, mudflats, beaches at low tide. That's why fishes flew and forests walked and the moon was blood. This small pebbledash cottage with the plastic chairs, at the further end of the Bettystown golf course, had once been a post office and she had been born there. And if she had been born there, her elder sisters must have been born there as well.

Did we walk down past the Maiden's Tower towards the sea-shelly banks of the larger river? I don't remember. Maybe I wondered again who was this maiden, was she related to the Nanny of the smaller river and the Betty of the forgettable holiday town. What I do remember was that I drove back to the boarded-up carnival, drove past the sweet shop onto the long, untidy stretch of beach that led to the barnacled walls of the mouth of the Boyne. I asked her did she want to walk and she said no, so I walked myself, down the sandy runnels of the retreating tide. I had the ungenerous, selfish thought that if the deflating dirigible of her holed heart gave out here it might bring her some comfort. Or some sense of completion. May the circle be unbroken. She had been born here, after all. Her mother had been a postmistress, probably sitting behind the steam-covered grille from which they served the coffee. Her father had probably jammed his easel into the sand dunes as he sketched the sails of the fishing boats crossing the bar. And what on earth was the bar? The spit of raised sand that the boats could get stuck on. There were two conical structures across the river that I could see now, beyond the waste of mussel shells. They looked ancient, built by nobody, or maybe by the bank of seaweed and barnacle shells they rose from. I could imagine barnacled hands, pushing them upwards. There must have been a name for them once. Maybe the Maiden knew it. There was a poem, by Tennyson. Crossing the bar? Sailing the bar? Moaning.

And may there be no moaning of the bar
When I put out to sea.

Could that sand bar moan? There was a low hum, of something. The Maiden, trapped in the tower. Or the electric pylons, in the dunes.

Double

Was there another life she could have lived? Of course. Where the father didn't die when she was young, where she studied in Paris instead of the Metropolitan School of Art, Dublin. Where she met Marc Chagall or Giacometti instead of Sean Keating and Maurice MacGonigal. Where she wasn't taken out of school to paint china cups in a porcelain factory in Marrowbone Lane. Where she never came across a national school teacher from the West of Ireland in a sou'wester, wheeling his bike through the falling rain

There's another life all of us could have lived, and what you don't know is did she ever imagine it. Did she walk down that Bray Promenade rattling her hand off the railings and imagine she was someone else, doing just that? Did she hop from paving stone to paving stone, avoiding the cracks and go, look at her there, hopping from one foot to the other, avoiding the cracks? Was it her life, but seemed like someone else's?

The way you did. And you realize that from an early age you always looked on your experiences as if they were someone else's. Even the act of looking. And the watcher and the watched could extend themselves forever, like the halls of mirrors they had in the Bettystown amusements. It seemed like a curse, when you were of an age to become aware of it. Jumping from paving stone to paving stone to avoid the cracks.

Was she sitting there, in the passenger seat of the car, wearing that red beret, watching the wind blow those scarves of sand from the sea, thinking, there is the sand again, blown in from the sea? Thinking there my eldest son goes, down towards the Boyne and the Maiden's Tower, leaving me here, wondering will I be alive when he gets back? Is there another Angela that lived in Paris, in the sixteenth arrondisement, remembering Marc Chagall instead of Sean Keating? Will heaven be like Gauguin's Tahiti? The sand at least would be softer there. Maybe, like you, she always needed a double. And that double needed a double and so on ad infinitum through that infinite hall of mirrors.

Jerusalem

Her own mother had worked for the Post Office in London when women constituted its main workforce, most of the male staff having enlisted. She had met her husband there, who hadn't enlisted and left in a hurry, around the time of the 1916 Rising. She was Irish. He, despite his name, O'Brien, was English. How could an O'Brien be English? Did he change his name? And why the hurry? Something to do with conscription, I was always told, Lord Kitchener's moustaches and accusing finger. Something to do with Michael Collins, who had worked in the same post office? I had aunts who swore that was the case. Or concluded that that must be the case. So I have to imagine her as a young Gaelic Leaguer wielding a hurley in a camogie game on the grounds of the Geraldine Athletic Club in Notting Hill. But the photographs that survive show someone too refined, too beautiful, for that. Maybe cheering from the sidelines? As the burly Collins shoulders aside her beloved? Which led to a fist fight and a reconciliation and pints in the Duke of Wellington on Portobello Road? Where certain Fenian oaths were exchanged? But he was a conscientious objector, not a gunman. The same postal service gave her a job here, above the Boyne river, so they can't have been running from the forces of the crown. But if that was the case, why the hurry? They had just married, the legend went, but didn't even take their wedding presents. He was a painter of some kind. He died young, left her mother with ten children and left her with an easel and some paintbrushes.

Her stories never really made sense. Or if they did make sense, the connective tissue was missing. Mother and kids hiding in the potato drills in the back garden from an army raid. What army? The Auxiliaries? The Black and Tans? One or other side in the Civil War? And was it here, outside the

Grandmother with teacup.   *Grandfather with cigarette.*

Mornington post office, with the wind flecking the Boyne waters far below?

They left Mornington on some unspecified date. A succession of houses, then, before they settled in Bray. The houses she would point out seemed impossibly grand, even palatial. But there was nothing palatial about this pebbledash two-storey coffee shop and nothing grand about a post office.

I had a dim memory of a stairway, hand-painted with a mural of an imaginary biblical landscape. Christ Weeps Over Jerusalem. A suitable theme, maybe, for the National Gallery, but for the peeling stairway of a house up from the Bray Promenade? But then, the hills above Jerusalem looked suspiciously like the hills above the Bray Promenade. Bray Head.

Her father riding a motorbike from Bray across the Sally Gap to where he worked, an art college in Dublin. Some memory of childhood bliss, and we all have those, interrupted by a tragedy. His sickness? Death? His dark-haired widow puts the family to work. The twins in a chemist's shop on Bray Main Street. She, in the porcelain factory, Marrowbone Lane. Painting decorative motifs on fine china. I imagine a Japanese parasol, a lady in a kimono crossing one of those ornamental bridges above an ornamental lake. Every brushstroke in fine china-blue.

Then there was the England he came from. Something to do with Cornwall, a mother named Sarah Salter (or was it Psalter?). There is a photograph of this Sarah, hunched and black-hatted with a rather elegant man beside her, holding a camera. Both seated by the railings of a promenade. Her husband, surely? But then who took the photograph? Her son? One camera photographs another. Where was that seascape? Land's End, Cornwall? Lyme Regis? Or Margate, where Turner painted all those puddled meetings of land and sea? Everything was a seascape around her. Everyone wore shades of black.

Photographs

So maybe I should start with the photographs. Of two grandfathers that I never met. And maybe that's why the word grandfather for me has an elusive, unexplored ring to it, like the Nanny, Betty and the mysterious Maiden. It comes with the scent of burning tobacco (my own father never smoked) and maybe that peaty odour of old-man tweed. But there is nothing peaty about the photograph of him, her father, holding a cat, in an elegant white shirt and a pair of Edwardian pants that button high towards the midriff. Who is this man and how different would I have been, had I been lucky enough to know him? He looks handsome, sophisticated and decidedly unIrish. Another photograph, again in the same unearthly white, holding a tennis racket. And again, those high-buttoned Edwardian pants.

The other grandfather, who looks like he never knew either end of a tennis racket, is photographed outside a thatched cottage, in a field in Roscommon, and has a button accordion round his neck. He could be a Russian serf on an estate owned by the Nabokov family. In fact he was a national school teacher, whose alcoholism led to an early death. He is smiling. They are both smiling. Everybody smiled then. Or was it just for photographs?

Grandfather with tennis racket and cat.

Two grandmothers I have met. One must have been married to the accordion-playing serf and if she terrified him as much as she terrified me, I can understand his attraction to alcohol. I used to dread the evenings when my parents went out and she 'minded' us. Minding me in particular meant making me finish my homework. None of my ingenious stratagems of avoidance would work with this lady. She would make me go through every sum, every misspelt word in Irish, until it was horribly, properly finished. She disapproved of me, for some impenetrable reason. I was bad at maths, which for her was probably reason enough.

The other died too young to teach me anything. I knew little of her apart from her photographs. The kind of unearthly beauty you find in Rossetti's paintings. My only memories of her are of a figure curled beneath blankets in an upstairs room in a grand house in Sydenham Villas, Bray. So this is where all that beauty goes. It shrivels, to end up surrounded by cough tissues. The children she left all populated the Bray and Greystones seafronts. Twins, who ran the chemist's shop on Main Street, which she managed to buy after her husband had died. Ita, who married Pearse and ran a boarding house by Greystones harbour, with a small sweet shop out the back. I used to stay with them some summers and dive off the harbour pier. Pearse, who was beguiled by an Indian fakir, who held a cigarette lit at both ends between his lips, who rolled around on broken glass on the sweet shop floor with his back bare to the glass. The fakir, not Pearse. I remember my uncle Pearse's description of his amazement, as if it was a story from the *Arabian Nights*.

The twins' chemist's shop was called Vance and Wilson, the name of which used to intrigue me. The twins, who were

O'Briens, Malachy and Eamon, wore identical grey smocks and had identical smiles but only one of them, Eamon, was my godfather. Somehow, I always recognized him. Neither of them was a Vance or a Wilson and I used to construct absurd fantasies and rhymes around the name, until one day Eamon solved the mystery for me. James Joyce's first love was an Eileen Vance, whose family owned the same shop. Because she was a Protestant, Joyce's aunt or grandmother, Dante – who must have been as terrifying as my paternal own – forbade any closer contact. It was all described – of course! – in a barely fictional form in *A Portrait of the Artist*.

Young Stephen Dedalus hides under the table, in number 1 Martello Terrace, down at the end of the promenade. Dante tells him eagles will pull out his eyes if he doesn't apologize.

> *Pull out his eyes,*
> *Apologise*

Maybe the twins were proud of the connection. Maybe they wanted to keep their Protestant clients. Maybe they were secret Joyceans. They never changed the name.

I can still remember that chemist's shop. The globules of glass around the counter, the ping as the door opened, the uncle twins, the loaf of bread-shaped lozenge sweets Eamon would give me. I always know it's your birthday, he would say, when I see the first lambs in the fields. The privileged trek behind the counter to their rooms upstairs. A strange innocence about everything. Eamon married first. In the way of those naive days, Marie, his beautiful wife, felt lucky she had two husbands to look after. Unaccountably happy, with her twins. So when the other twin married, someone had to go. Life kicked in. Paradise is always lost.

Pearse and Ita vanished soon afterwards, to a life for him as a commercial traveller in Glasgow. My mother later told me dark tales of a mysterious man who gained some devilish hold over him, managed to con him out of whatever money he had. Could it have been the same fakir who lit a cigarette at both ends (it must have been untipped) and placed it vertically between his lips? Who crushed the empty lemonade bottles with a concrete block, and walked barefoot across the broken shards, before stripping to his underwear and rolling back and forwards over them on his unbloodied back? Was the burning cigarette still between his lips?

All of these questions.

Anyway, the fakir took Pearse's money and he sold the boarding house and the sweet shop and was condemned, like a medieval penitent, to years of wandering. They ended up in a cottage in the same Bettystown, where he built the ship that would never reach the Azores, near the post office in Mornington where my mother, apparently, was born.

Like my vanished grandfathers, nothing entirely made sense. Were this debonair painter and his Pre-Raphaelite beauty of a wife on the run for political reasons? They looked nothing like Collins's working-class squad. Liam Tobin was never photographed with a tennis racket, in high-waisted buttoned white pants.

Ita died in the kitchen of that cottage. At her funeral Pearse described how she fell and he reached out his arms to catch her, but before she reached them she was in the arms of someone else. His romanticism was persuasive and overwhelming. He threw a single white rose into her grave.

He got married again, eventually, to an elegant woman who dressed him in herringbone tweed. Maybe he was afflicted, like Van Morrison's Madame George, with the love that loves to love.

And later, when he fell on hard times, Pearse sold me the last of my grandfather's remaining pictures. A wizened old man, lighting a church candle.

Alternative History

There was an Ireland that didn't exist yet and I came to live in it. The one that was ending might have been better and I'd love to write a book one day on what it could have been. The Home Rule Act is passed despite the outbreak of the First World War. The Irish Parliamentary Party wins the 1918 election and the island as a whole become a dull, obedient partner in the wider British Empire. Georgian Dublin is destroyed by the Luftwaffe, and not by rapacious developers from Offaly and Cavan, anywhere beyond the Pale. John Lennon grows up in Donabate and Paul McCartney in Greystones. They meet on the 45 bus and Beatlemania spreads from the Grove in Clontarf to conquer the world.

And still this painter makes the journey across, he's a conscientious objector, he evades the accusing finger of Lord Kitchener in this little post office above the Boyne river. And I imagine these two grandfathers meeting. I can't help it. Where? At the race meeting in Laytown, where else? The small horses running, what do they call them? Flappers. The elegant grandfather enjoying the spectacle, of this Ireland he has come to appreciate, celebrate, reacquaint himself with. O'Brien was his name after all. He has a cane, dressed in those high-waisted pants. There is a woman with him, of course, wearing a wide-brimmed hat. They are in the first flush, or confusion, of their honeymoon. Maybe even call it love. The horses are raising sheets of water from the incoming tide, the jockeys bent forwards, skinny kids from traveller caravans up and down the coastline, from as far away as Limerick and Listowel. A sense of ancient anarchy behind the crowd, this isn't the West, after all, this is the turbulent hinterland of Drogheda, and there's a pagan energy behind it all; the Boyne river two miles up the beach stretches into the Valley of the Kings. And there's a sound accompanying the spectacle, the flapping colours, the thundering hooves and the horsewhips. It could be a sailor's melodeon, but no, it's a button accordion, the kind they actually play in the West, a difficult instrument, an intake of the bellows plays one note and an express on the same bellows plays another. And it's the other grandfather, the one from Roscommon, Boyle, Elphin, he's lost his teaching job, alcohol has taken him far from home and he's reduced to this, playing for pennies at a flapper race meeting. Or maybe not. Maybe he's playing for the fun of it, has brought his young son across counties to enjoy this spectacle, the horses running along the low tide at Laytown beach and he's brought his accordion for enjoyment.

It was a small country, why not? Laytown wasn't that far from Elphin, Co. Roscommon. And if anyone could have been part of Collins's squad it would have been this entrancing squeezebox player. But of course he was more sophisticated than that accordion. One of the earliest pictures of my father is of him holding a violin outside a schoolhouse, in short pants

Watercolour, Laytown Races, Angela Jordan.

with his own father's string quartet. His own father holds a cello. How did he move from the squeezebox to the cello, from the thatched cottage to the schoolhouse lawn?

Somehow the Englishman seems familiar, the Irishman as foreign as if he's stepped from the pages of Dostoevsky or Gogol. Or Somerville and Ross, describing a peasantry they can barely comprehend. But the question still is why. Why did the Englishman return; how had he got there in the first place? Was it a homecoming or a departure? He had studied painting in a place called Strawberry Hill, a name which seems to fit with those high-waisted Edwardian pants and that billowing shirt. His mother's name was a Sarah Salter. Or Psalter. There is a deliciously biblical resonance to the latter, and it makes me think of prayer books and the Plymouth Brethren. Maybe they ran a business printing bibles. But no, her family were wheelwrights, in Cornwall, not in Plymouth. So let's stick with Salter, make it a child's rhyme. By the sea sits Sarah Salter. Her husband sits beside her, on the iron-wrought seat, camera in hand. It's the camera that confuses, demands an explanation. But it's there, without a doubt. And who took that photograph? Their son, surely, who became the painter.

Ireland's Own

He made money for a time doing illustrations for Irish children's histories, and nationalist publications like *Ireland's Own*. Did he share in their naivety, like those other gullible Englishmen, Roger Casement and Erskine Childers?

A few of the illustrations have survived – Fenians with long braided hair and conical bras like Madonna would one day delight in (or were they breastplates?) pointing at an estuary that looked suspiciously like the mouth of the Boyne river, from a vantage point that could well have been the Mornington post office. These were Fenians of the Diarmuid and Gráinne, not the De Valera or Michael Collins kind. And up the river are sailing what seem to be Viking longships. So maybe he had a workroom at the back of the post office, and a view of the mouth of the river that led towards Tara and the Valley of the Kings. Or a shed among the potato drills where his children would later hide from whatever armed forces were searching the same post office. But where did the other story come from, that my mother would let slip, like someone dreaming of a past life? Of the shellfish co-operative? I would spend hours walking up and down the Boyne, climbing the excrement-smelling

Maiden's Tower, looking down on the nets pulling in salmon from the mouth of the river. There were fishermen then, too, half a century before, eking out a living from the salmon runs. This enterprising painter, son of a photographer and wheelwright's daughter from Cornwall, gathered them together into a shellfish co-operative and shipped molluscs to the English coast. They loved shellfish, you see, those English he had fled from, all the villages in Kent, from Southend to Hastings to Margate, where Turner had painted the half-bloody sunrise on the beach and somebody, when Turner was long dead, had named it *Sunrise with Sea Monsters*. They loved cockles, mussels, whelks, periwinkles, all of those shells the Boyne fisherman crushed beneath their boots as they threw nets for the elusive salmon. So there was an enterprise, apparently, that thrived, and an early version of a socialist collective, which I found hard to connect with the elegantly dressed tennis player on the Bray Promenade. And neither could I find any corroborating accounts of the above tale, from aunts, uncles, sisters and brothers. But I swear my mother told it to me. Maybe she was a fantasist as well. Maybe fantasy is better than reality.

Of course the post office where they met was London. Burnished brass railings around the room, small barred windows behind which the postmistresses sat. The brass railings like the ones in Mornington, like golden prison bars, from which a pair of bored brown eyes – no, not brown, blue or hazel-flecked green, observe the besuited figures of the men that came and went. One of them, apparently, was Michael Collins. He wouldn't have done anything like sit in the sorting office. No, he delivered mail, on his bicycle, round the grand houses of Kensington when he wasn't cycling to play hurley

Illustration, Eamon O'Brien.

with his beloved friend Harry Boland, latter-day Fenians both of them, without the conical brassieres.

So an art student walks in one day wearing tweed, the sleeves of the linen shirt spattered with paint. He would have kept the sleeves tucked behind the rougher sleeves of the tweed jacket. He wants to send a postcard to Sarah Salter, his mother back in Cornwall. He is a dutiful son and does things like that. The assistant hands him the stamp, takes his money and gives him the change. Does she glance at the image on the front as he licks it? No knowing, of course, but let's have her do that. Even better, let's have her throw her eyes over the broad handwriting on the other side. Your loving son. And she likes him for that, who wouldn't, as she watches him fix the wetted stamp to the delineated square space assigned for it and drop it with a dull cardboard rustle into the post box that sits like a plinth in the middle of the black-and-white-tiled floor. Michael Collins won't deliver that one, no, he only does the Kensington round, but maybe he has double duties, has to, at the end of the day, fill a canvas sack with the deposited letters, postcards and all and trundle them down to the horse-drawn post van waiting outside.

Or maybe it wasn't like that at all. On her weekends she cycled out to Strawberry Hill where he gave Saturday painting classes. Or maybe it was an arranged match: a father in Ireland writes to an acquaintance in London for a suitable prospective husband, they walk around those lush green parks with the harsh tree shadows defining each and every step, followed by two governesses in dark-green late-Victorian triangular cloaks. Or even better, on a trip down to Lyme Regis – even trainee assistant postmistresses can buy a ticket on the train, can't they? – she is walking with a girlfriend – let's call her Sally, Sally is as convivial and unthreatening a name as you'll get, Sally is always an ideal friend and who could imagine a rival in looks, bearing, sensuality and beauty called Sally? – above those proverbial pines and there is an itinerant photographer there, taking pictures of the holidaymakers for a small fee. He has a tripod, a plate camera, a hooded piece of velvet to protect the negative from random sunbeams. He is penniless, of course, having spent all his money on his photographic home studio and offers his services. No, more than offers, he begs to be hired, has been standing there all day with his black box and uncomfortable boots and his frayed three-piece suit, waistcoat and all, since one has to look respectable to earn a penny without being arrested, and the business has been as evanescent as those chemical plates he has so carefully stacked beside him. She is away from London for the weekend and all of the tedious grind of keeping the Empire's threads of communication moving and she has some money to spare and, yes, she would like her photograph taken with her friend Sally who will provide no unwelcome contrast to her own beauty. But maybe it's not like that; again, Sally is the beauty, Sally has money to burn and all the time in the world to spare, and Sally hires the itinerant photographer in the full confidence that her Irish acquaintance, barely above a chambermaid as she is, would not provide an unwelcome contrast to her own widely acknowledged charms.

So Sally agrees the price and the itinerant photographer asks for a moment of stillness, against the railings with the burned-out sea behind and vanishes beneath his dusty velvet tent of black. But underneath there something happens. He examines the ground glass or looks through the eyepiece and sees them both: Sally, her head thrown artificially back, with a smile that displays her perfect teeth, and her companion looks straight at him with a darkness that she seems to have carried with her and it is that darkness, surrounded by the tousled darkness of her unbound hair, that makes him catch his breath. He presses the button and the phosphorous ignites and the silver nitrate on the plate catches the moment, and catches that darkness too. There is an exchange of money, and a card, and a promise to deliver the finished print to the Excelsior Hotel and the print is duly delivered, not by him, but by his son. The son is tall, like the father, but with much more ambition and without a waistcoat or even a jacket. He wears a loose-sleeved white shirt and a pair of elegant trousers, buttoned high, to the midriff. He delivers the finished prints of course not to Sally, but to her, the dark Irish one. And for some reason he is holding a cat.

Nobody remembers this, because it didn't happen. But there is one memory that I know is mine. Of the house in Sydenham Villas, an ungainly Victorian pile beneath Bray Head with its staircase that seemed bigger than any staircase I had ever climbed (we lived in a house without one at the time) with its huge fresco of a mountain outside Jerusalem up the staircase wall and the figure of an idealized Christ (who looked alarmingly like the Fenian, pointing at the oncoming Viking longships) gesturing at the city below. Christ Weeps Over Jerusalem. Did he paint it on the wet plaster, the way the Florentines did? I doubt it. But I remember it. I would walk slowly up the enormous staircase, past this sunlit, idealized landscape, to pay my childhood respects to his widow, who was dying upstairs.

And, I wonder, are memories like this, as you get older, sit alone in a car looking out on the metal-green Irish Sea, towards the seaweed-green pillars at the mouth of the Boyne, the brown hills of Baltray beyond and the Mourne Mountains beyond them again, as your son walks back towards you through the twisting runnels of sand. They come and go, like September breezes and what is real is not as important as what is imaginary. So a shellfish co-operative where Viking marauders in longships once sailed after a flight from a London post office becomes not too outlandish. Everything turns into everything else. We all end up in the same dim mist. Her brother Malachy was killed by the spare wheel that bounced off the back of a lorry and crushed him by the privet hedge of his front garden. Her response was, he's gone to meet his twin.

The tide is coming in and I have to pick my way through the salt pools, and can see the wind is blowing them against the wheels of my car. I can see the shape through the misted window, the red beret motionless over the green cardigan. I wonder has she gone to meet both twins, and open the door gently to find she's just been asleep. And I drive her back down the beach past the shuttered carnival and home.

Memoir

I'm sure we all wish we had other childhoods. To be Tom Sawyer, getting random passersby to paint his fence. To be Smith of the Remove, robbing Billy Bunter's tuck. In fact Greyfriars School and St Petersburg, Missouri, seem more familiar to me than the world of my own childhood. I must have always wanted some escape. It was so strange, yet so ordinary. The rules were so fixed, and yet they made no sense whatsoever. They seemed to have always been there, but they couldn't have been, could they, since they vanished almost imperceptibly, without leaving any trace, like children's rhymes that refer to things you never knew about. Asha, asha, we all fall down. Something to do with the war, though we didn't go through it. Something to do with the Catholicism which pervaded everything like the smell of wood varnish in a nunnery. And the only approximation, the only sense of familiarity I found to that world of my childhood was when I visited the states behind what used to be, as we called it, with a sense of futuristic dread, 'the Iron Curtain'. Bucharest, Budapest, Prague, Tbilisi. There was the same sense of an illogical glue that held the whole furniture of existence together that suddenly vanished. A populace of denim-clad kids so eager to embrace new freedoms that they almost destroyed themselves. Beautiful cities, ravaged by the grossest kind of discarded modernity. The brutalist architecture of the sixties and seventies looming over medieval and always somehow brown streets. And the unspoken question, everywhere, what the hell was that all about?

And maybe I've no reason to write this story. Because I wasn't raped, abandoned, sent to a reformatory, abused by relatives unknown. I didn't go to rehab, find the Lord, learn the Serenity Prayer.

Because despite a tangled childhood, things were generally OK. Because I was indeed beaten by priests with long straps we called leathers, but managed to survive. Because my father once – and only once, as far as I remember – whacked me with an open palm outside a small cottage in Connemara and I sailed across one of those dry stone walls, but was more astounded by the propulsive force behind the gesture than the pain it caused. But, then, he had been a handball player in his youth and as my mother always said, 'there are good goods in small parcels'. Did this refer to some strange sexual gymnastics he could practise in private? Or to the fact that he was, admittedly, small? I will never know. But that's OK, too.

Likbez

Where she met him, I have no idea. He had been studying maths at Galway University. Mathematics was to be a constant in his life, so I must have been a great disappointment to him. There was some kind of crisis, a breakdown or an illness, so he changed courses and studied teacher training. The painterly grandfather ran the art classes there, was it St Pat's in Drumcondra, where he ended up, teaching the teachers who would eventually teach me? Again, I have no idea. But he met the daughter of the painter, got his first job in Sligo and would cycle from there to meet her and take her to the pictures in O'Connell Street.

Cycle from Sligo? Surely I've got that wrong. Google Maps makes it a ten-hour journey. But that was the legend, a newly qualified teacher, with a job in Rosses Point, dripping wet in a cycling cape and rain gear, taking the young daughter of the painter on a first date. Maybe he cycled to the Sligo train station, and then from the station in Kingsbridge as it was then called, along the Liffey. The rain spattering the brown water and washing the statue of Daniel O'Connell clean of its patina of birdshit. Down to the Pillar, which is shrouded in the same downpour he had left in Rosses Point. Where she waits, sheltered in the stone doorway. Or underneath Clerys' clock. To the Carlton, probably, where as well as watching a 'picture' you could have tea and cakes and even waltz to an orchestra in the upstairs ballroom.

There is a photograph of them ascending the steps of an aircraft, on their honeymoon. He is in a belted overcoat, she in a tweed suit, a breeze fanning out her hair, sultry with happiness. For some reason she reminds me of Eva Braun. I know I should be thinking Humphrey Bogart and Lauren Bacall, the plane looks the same as the one in *Casablanca*, but, no, the image of Eva Braun won't leave my brain, the way a bad pop song can stick there, regurgitating its dreadful lyric. He looks nothing like Adolf Hitler, has no moustache, the belted macintosh looks American, if anything, but his hair is parted in the middle and brilliantined down, very much the way the Führer liked to wear his. So is that the connection? Or does everyone think their father has a shadow self? He had magazines upstairs, I would discover, on the educational theories of the National Socialists and the Corporate State, but they, I am sure, were a necessity at the time to anyone studying education as a discipline. He had also treatises on Friedrich Froebel and Maria Montessori, and on Vladimir Lenin's policy of Likbez ('the liquidation of illiteracy'). He would come to rewrite the entire junior curriculum with the education minister, Donogh O'Malley, so his own practice was far more enlightened than those of Lenin's Likbez or of the Nationalsozialistischer Lehrerbund; maybe the autosuggestive image says more about me than him. But he never reminded me of Vladimir Ilich. Did every child fear their father resembled the Führer? Or even more terrifying, worry that their father secretly was the Führer? We would play war games as kids, and in a strange upending of sympathies, the most glamorous, most popular, most handsome (what would be known now as the coolest) children always got to be the Nazis. Their uniforms were better, the helmets to die for – they even had flame throwers, for God's sake – and I, being meek, mild and decidedly uncool, would play the lowly Brit. Who always lost, incidentally. Or was brought before some mock trial and condemned to some Teutonic punishment. So maybe that's where the Eva Braun image came from?

But no, in the end it's none of these. It was the utter, unthinking devotion in her face. He could have been Alexander the Great, Ivan the Terrible or Vladimir Ilich Lenin. She still would have followed him.

Rosses Point

They honeymooned in London or Paris, or maybe both, and returned to the windswept slopes underneath Ben Bulben. Rosses Point, where he taught in a one-teacher school. I was born there. I have an image of a small, sandy road leading to the sea and the camel's hump of an island beyond. That would have been Coney Island, and not the one with the Ferris wheels and the colourful mobsters and the endless beach packed with attractive bathers, watched over by the yellow towers of the life-savers. No, this was the first Coney Island, 4,000 miles away. A sort of plinth in the bay, with a metal man, a sailor with one arm always pointing in the same direction. A lighthouse? No, it was one of those barnacled towers that guide ships towards the Sligo docks. So they can once more 'cross the bar'. A vista that Jack Yeats could have painted, and indeed did. That my mother definitely painted, so my memory could have been of one of her watercolours or oils, and not of the bay itself. She kept painting, like her father before her. She would eventually have to supplement the family income by painting small, idealized images of the West of Ireland for tourist shops, two inches by four, inside mass-produced frames, always with the same image: a donkey and creel walking away from or towards a bog, accompanied by a shawled lady. Turf stacked on the creel. A cottage in the background, thatched, of course, with a stack of turf at the gable end. Was it an Ireland she ever saw? But then again, did her grandfather ever see Viking longships on the Boyne river? It was an Ireland that De Valera so grandiloquently described, that tourists wanted. She came to hate the practice, the paintings, but always liked turf and donkeys, Coney Island and the metal man with the immobile arm.

She gave it up finally and went back to what she liked doing best, painting the real world in front of her. Watercolours, oils, a kind of unravelling home movie of the life we lived.

Geese and I at Rosses Point.

I could invent memories, but they would probably be false. I wish I had a traumatic childhood to report, full of hysterical misery, but all I can remember is its opposite, and it wasn't what Freud so glumly termed ordinary unhappiness. It was brushed with the soft edges and the nostalgic mist of her drawings. All of the colours muted. I have a sense of sitting in a pram with the crumbling taste of Goldgrain biscuits somewhere on my tongue, looking at the same scene. A row of cottages with a metal gate, roses tumbling round it and Coney Island and the metal man beyond. There was a pub called Austy's, to the left of it, which my father would have never visited because he didn't drink. There was a one-teacher school, somewhere in the hinterland, where he could explore all of his educational theories. There was a choir (always a choir) which he organized. Which makes me think of the rather forlorn image of him as a child holding a violin with other members of that adult string quartet, somewhere in Boyle or Elphin. Elphin. Even the name has a mythological ring to it, making me think of elves and Greece and mountains in Tibet. Did his father, the squeezebox-playing teacher, play the cello or the viola? Whence all this sophistication? My mother's phrase, describing her diminutive husband. There are good goods in small parcels. The goods and the parcel were hers.

They moved from this paradise to Dublin soon after, and that's when my memories really began. Wilson Road in Stillorgan, another drab cottage with a garden at the back. Poplar trees, pointing like dark-green candles towards a cloudy sky. There was a childminder who looked after us, and I can still remember her long dark hair as she reached down to pick me up. The strands of her hair like the poplar trees behind them. She was in love with me and I with her. I was in love with everyone then. She reached down into the grass beneath the poplar trees and picked something up. What was it, I had to know. A leprechaun, she said, and showed me one finger twisted on her other palm, with a small glove puppet. It bowed its head in recognition and spoke a word or two. I saw a leprechaun, I told my mother, in the small kitchen at the end of the cement garden walk. Never, she said, her Eva Braun hair bent over the sink and her hands full of suds. Why were her hands always full of suds? Why were there no stairs in the house? Why did she hate it so?

I must have learned to walk, with one of those stirrup or reins things and so lost my first love, that dangling brown hair and the soft hands that hid the leprechaun and picked me out of the pram. I even made a friend, who turned out to be Dermot Morgan who later became Father Ted. I remember a bike with stabilizers, and she led me down an avenue with sycamore trees, called, rather predictably, Trees Road, to the beach near Blackrock. The waves cold and uninviting, the twin towers of the pigeon house beyond. I longed to swim when the tide was out, the sun illuminating all of the little sculpted shells of sand. She made me promise never to cycle there on my own. But I did, of course, on my own or with the baby Father Ted, and saw the low tide, almost to the horizon, the sun illuminating a million tiny glittering pools. I cycled back, of course and told her the tide was out, the conditions perfect, and begged her to take me swimming. How do you know? she asked. Someone told me, I lied, a pathetic lie, and I blushed of course which made the lie even more evident. Was it my first?

A first lie, like a first love, can never be forgotten. So it must have been. More lies followed, of course, and I got no better at them. Another friend's father was a commercial traveller who dealt in Canadian cigarettes that went by the name of Black Cats – and I can still see the black cat peering over the top of the packet. We used to steal them in packets, though we did nothing so adventurous as smoke them. No, we laid them out in rows, lit one end and watched them burn. Have you been lighting matches, she asked me on my return. No, I lied. Then why are your eyelashes burned?

There was a school then, where I learned not to lie. Or how to really lie. It must have been a pre-school, I know it was a Montessori. Nuns, with white bonnets, bending over. The women in my childhood always bent over. I must have been small, and accepted their obeisance as a recompense for the loss of the brown hair. There was a tree, a sycamore or an oak, in the centre of a gravelled garden. I played with sand and coloured blocks, either there or in a conservatory into which the sunlight seemed always to be streaming. Did the nuns bring the idea of goodness, bliss and an all-loving God? One should never introduce the idea of God to a child. Like leprechauns, they can only take it literally. I wore a first communion smock, like an altar boy. Maybe I was an altar boy? No, that came later. There is a photograph by the sycamore tree, of a boy with lank hair and brown eyes that must have been me. Hands joined together, in a steeple shape, an imitation of prayer. Or were they even nuns? Maybe they were beings from another world. Sisters of consolation who didn't wear bonnets, the halos round their bending heads came from the sunshine pouring through the leaves of the sycamore tree.

43

But they shouldn't have told me about God. Or Heaven. Because I went from Heaven to Hell then, and it seemed instantaneous. I passed from pre-school to the first year of primary, to the Christian Brothers down the road. An immediate explosion of brutality, and a world that obeyed radically different rules. The logic in this new order seemed to be a day structured around beatings, and with my own child's need for order, I had to accept it. You walked down the road with the trees to the red-brick mausoleum (or were you walked? By mother or father, or by one of those celestial beings who had to pass you on into the shadows?) and entered a classroom with forty or so other children. The entire class then lined up in front of a figure in black, who took an object from beneath his black skirt. These men wore skirts for some reason, skirts under which you could occasionally glimpse the line of creased trousers. This object was called a leather, and was indeed made of leather, studded with small brass buttons. You held out your hands and the leather whistled through the air, nine or ten times, the force of the blow bringing tears to your eyes, red stripes to your hand, and necessitating a rise and fall of those country boots worn from the parquet floor. The effort of the blow lifted them. With a squeak of leather up, and a clack of heel down. So there were three sounds to this procedure, the whistle, the whack and the clack. The floor was immaculate, golden and shiny. It had seen decades of this ritual. You then shuffled on, lining the walls of the classroom while others behind you observed the same ritual. There was a certain sense to it, you realized. Punishment normally followed an infraction. But since infractions were inevitable (there were rules, too many of them to fully get a handle on) why not dole out the punishment before the infraction had actually happened? You were beaten, you took your place behind the small wooden desk and then instruction began. There was a logic to the system, even a warped kind of genius, you had to admit. Time was turned on its head. The punishment fitted the crime, although the crime hadn't happened yet. And the fact that punishment had been given, and received, was no protection against further punishments throughout the day, which had not yet begun. In fact it was a cast-iron guarantee of the same. And you have barely noticed the fact that in the telling, you have moved from the first-person singular to the second. Because this world, with its warped logic and demonic sense of order was imposing itself on someone else, not me. Was happening to someone else, not you.

You have already begun the process of separation from the self. But the real question is, who did you tell about it? Your mother, who you already suspect hates this concrete suburb and longs for her lost paradise of Coney Island and the metal man? (And she was not Eva Braun at all now, nor was she Lauren Bacall, she was stressed and distracted, like Maureen O'Hara in that West of Ireland cottage before John Wayne comes in and drags her by the hair.) Your father, who walked up the sycamore-lined road as the day was ending, with his umbrella swinging? It seemed unkind to bother them, and more than unkind, dangerous. You must, after all, have done something to deserve such punishment. But, and here the real problem lay, you could never work out what. What was the infraction, what was the crime, what was the original sin?

Traps

They were both released soon after. We moved, my sister, my brother and I, across the bay to the north side of the river. Clontarf, a middle-class suburb in a sea of council houses. A semi-detached, on the corner of Baymount Park, 243 Mount Prospect Avenue, overlooking St Anne's Estate. She was happier there. How could I tell? I don't know, but children have a sense of such things. The sea was closer for one thing. There was a bridge, leading to the Bull Wall, made of old railway sleepers that rumbled as the cars moved over them, and a long stretch of beach called Dollymount Strand. There was the 30 bus that idled on the corner, emitting clouds of petrol fumes. There was a shop down the end of the road, managed by a man with a stiff leg and a strange toupee.

And there was a bunch of kids on the road that came knocking one day.

There's someone here for you, she said in the new kitchen, which had a red and white tablecloth with triangular squares. I walked out and hovered by the staircase. We had one, finally, and I could happily bump down it on the hall mat for hours.

Four or five faces, by the front door. Boys my age.

It's a trap, I told her.

Why would it be a trap? she asked.

My head must have been full of tangled webs, of stories of abduction, capture, hidden webs that would jerk into action, pulled by an unleashed branch from above, and in an explosion of dead leaves, leave you hanging underneath. Yes, of course it was a trap, and the ruse was to pull me into it. There was a park across the way with an unused football pitch and beyond that a wilderness of forest with a strange ornamental lake, moss-covered Grecian gazebos and a magnificent Victorian ruin, the roof of which had fallen in, exposing the walls of separate floors. An overgrown ornamental maze surrounded by high walls, again like something out of *Great Expectations*. It had been a Guinness mansion, burned in the forties and left to decay. The whole place was a savage garden, with overgrown trees that had accrued legendary titles. One was called the Elephant's Arse, with huge bulbous encrustations of bark and a dark hole you could crawl into, if you didn't mind the terror of confinement in an elephant's interior. And everything smelled of dead leaves and excrement. These kids shitted everywhere, from the crumbling staircase that led into what once must have been an elegant bedroom, down into the depths of a scullery below. Maybe they just wanted to leave their mark.

Nobody died, which was extraordinary, as we explored the ruin, salvaged pieces of metal from the wreckage, climbed the broken staircase, edged our way along what remained of the upper floors. The garden frightened us far more than the building did, with its high walls overburdened with ivy and its rusting metal doors. It seemed designed for ghosts, that place, and on the few times I made my way inside it I imagined them everywhere. A girl in a white dress, always just out of my vision in the topiary maze. A caretaker with a tall black hat, just a shadow until the sun went down.

Across the park was Raheny and other bands of kids, tougher than us. We all attended Belgrove School, on Seafield Road, and I received an inkling there as to my father's mysterious occupation. He taught the teachers who taught me.

So that was this new world. The 30 bus spewing its fumes on the end of Baymount Park. To the right, the walk down to the stretch of water and the tufted dunes of Dollymount Strand beyond it. The old black wooden staves of the wooden bridge sinking into the same water. The sound of the railway sleepers shifting as the cars trundled over. The stretch towards infinity of the Bull Wall, with a cement Virgin Mary towering over the infinite. Maybe that's what she was, an invitation to infinity. But there was a stretch of the bay beyond, through which the ferries would pass and the East Wall to the right and another wall beyond on the south side which led to the Poolbeg lighthouse. Maybe it's when you become aware of yourself as a separate person that you wonder how did I ever get here. This landscape seems such an odd one to have fallen into. There must be another one somewhere, into which you would have fitted more neatly, more naturally, maybe even into one of those vistas your mother painted on miniature canvasses, with always a boy and a girl, generally barefoot, following a donkey laden with turf towards a thatched cottage. There would be a wisp of smoke coming from the cottage chimney and a woman waiting, wrapped round in a shawl. A lake, or the distant jagged inlet of the Atlantic sea. Perhaps you were that boy and your sister was that girl, but, no, this was no idealized memorial, she painted these by the dozen for the shops that sold tweed caps to tourists on Grafton Street. How it was long, long ago, how it used to be. And maybe that's what all fairy tales are about. I could have been someone somewhere else. A prince, or at the very least the emperor of some bed of nettles other than this one. There is a melody that will come drifting in round the tangled woods of St Anne's Estate that will lead me to it. Some day my prince will come. A pair of reddened lips that will kiss me back to a proper life. Because this could hardly be it, could it? This cul-de-sac where the kids played soccer on the street until their mothers called them in. You were defined by your ability to tap that ball around. By that, and your father's car. My father for a long time didn't have a car and when it finally arrived it was a second-hand one with rusting doors and the windscreen wipers never worked. But at least I had a father. Two boys my age who hadn't got one were punished mercilessly, hourly, daily, relentlessly by the gang of kids who ran Baymount Park. One was adopted and his adoptive father was a captain of the tugboats that led the container ships out of Dublin Bay. He would take us out there, an adventure, onto the wet granite cobblestones underneath the dockland gantries, onto a small tugboat that he guided, with a pipe between his teeth and some kind of sailor's hat, leading the huge metal prow of whatever cargo ship needed guiding, then somewhere after the Poolbeg lighthouse, turn around, back towards the yellow gantries that soared above the distant port. Or were they red? The kind of russet colour that prevents oxidization? I can't remember. What I do remember is that on the drive home he would stop outside the Yacht pub, leave us in the car while he vanished behind the round porthole window that decorated the pub door. We would wait, patiently at first. I had waited for adults before, but never outside a pub door, in a Morris Minor thick with stale cigarette smoke, the mist of our children's breath on the windows gradually obscuring the street outside. And never so long. Hours seemed to pass, with the misted shapes of adults passing, too, the sound of the pub door flapping, which the son hoped would be the tugboat adoptive father making his way out. We could have walked home, and I began to wonder why he hadn't told us to, instead of condemning us to this airless incarceration. Then eventually the door opened and he got back in. The lower lip tucked beneath the upper as if to obscure something. Whatever it was, it wasn't pleasurable. The inhale and the sharper exhale through his nostrils. He didn't want us to smell his breath. I said nothing, but could feel that Sean, his son, was in the state of a spring that had been coiled too long. His head began to bounce off the car ceiling as we drove the few hundred yards home. Inside the house in Baymount Park, his mother greeted us and the coiled spring effect continued. Boing, boing, boing, like a cartoon kid bouncing off the banisters. What happened next was like a cartoon, too, but one I had never seen before. The father whips off his coat, his jacket, down to his serge sailor's waistcoat and grabs the wooden coat hanger and instead of inserting it into the sleeves of his coat and jacket, begins to beat his son, mercilessly. The kid runs to the kitchen, the mother calls no, Sean, which is when I realized they are both called Sean. The kitchen door slams, and there is some punishing business in the garden; when the front door whips open again, the son runs in and up the stairs, the father following, the coat hanger by now reduced to splinters. Which is when I make my exit through the mercifully open door.

I had a trick in this mad garden. Maybe it was a stratagem of survival. I could take any amount of punishment, but never dole it out. Could ask other kids to punch me in the stomach, which I learned to tighten, like a sheet of metal. Could climb to the highest branch and drop like a stone, and tumble before my knees cracked into my lower jaw and shattered my teeth. I could become emperor in this bed of nettles. And this emperor would observe this other in his unfortunate exile in St Anne's Estate, on Dollymount Strand.

The one would watch the other's behaviour with a jaded, jaundiced and distressingly objective eye. Now he is doing this. Now he is sitting down by the sand dune, watching the sand pour through his fingers. Now he is walking down the Bull Wall watching for the wind blowing the skirts of the girls in front of him. Now he is counting the slabs on the pavement, walking towards the National Museum with his father, mother, sister and brother, hoping that the total number of steps when they reach the great oak door will be divisible by three. Now he is waiting by Nelson's Pillar, wondering does he have enough money to play the cinematic jukebox in Funland when he takes time to wonder about the neon sign: Come In And Have Fun In Funland, and a dapper gent approaches him from behind. Would he like a cigarette? Of course he would, although he didn't really smoke, and when the silver cigarette case is popped open – or clicked, really, it opens with a click to reveal a row of neat Sweet Aftons held in place by a silk band. The dapper gent's eyes were young and old at the same time, young because of their startling blue and old because of the tiny lines creased around them. Why are these young-old gents always coming up to him, generally from behind, as if they had time to observe him, like the other, somewhere in his brain, behind his own eyes. But he has a violin case with him, and has to make his way up Grafton Street to the School of Music where the portly violin teacher will peel mandarin oranges as he goes through his scales. He will come to hate the smell of mandarin oranges and the violin neck, and long for frets similar to the one on his miniature guitar and come to skip the classes, wander the stalls of Woolworths instead, pocketing anything that comes into his view until a voice whispers into his ear, I saw that little number, put it back now or I'll lock you in the cupboard inside. So he puts it back, because he doesn't want to be locked in the cupboard inside and he'll go instead to his imprisonment in Dollymount.

Fathers

It was a punishing place, that Baymount Park, but, oddly, it only seemed to punish those with absent, or ersatz fathers. How the kids recognized this difference I had no idea. Sean wore the same kinds of clothes that I did, had the same scratched knees, had a mother, who, apparently, loved him. Kevin, up the bend of the road, had a mother that visited him around Christmas, but for the most part was in the care of his elder brother and his childless uncle and aunt. And again, the recognition of this absence was immediate, permanent and merciless. What was it about fathers, I wondered, that mattered so much? Or was it just any difference, any departure from the norm? Kevin at least had wit, had a merciless, scathing tongue that gave him some kind of protection. Sean had none. Most of those games, on the Gaelic pitch, before the soccer took over, involved elaborate stratagems of punishment, for him alone. Condemned to twenty-four lashes. I object. Objection over-ruled. I object to the overruling. Condemned to twelve more. One elaborate game of fantasy involving knights or Nazis or Apaches and bounty hunters left him hanging beneath an ornamental bridge, with the rope so entwined around his shoulders and his neck that he was slowly and actually being strangled. It must have been knights, since the bridge and the gothic tower above it were part of the series of follies with which the Guinness owners had once decorated the park. Whatever it was, the rules of the game invited this medieval punishment. I propped up his knees as they heard his mother's voice coming through the woods. She untangled him from above and cursed them as monsters.

Were they monsters? They would have happily killed him, I was aware of that. They would grow up to be car salesmen, advertising executives, shopkeepers, solicitors, play for Manchester United (under 21s).

Kevin had one friend, me. Being a Dunne, he was nicknamed Mucky. (All Dunnes were called Mucky, for some impenetrable reason.) He had an older brother who would chase him down to the Clontarf Road with his belt strap swinging in the air. Passing my father, saying, I'm sorry Mr Jordan, can't stop now. Tell Neil I'll see him later.

Did the brother ever catch him? He must have, his legs were longer.

He had an uncle and aunt who used to drink some green cocktail at Christmas time. He had a mother in England who taught the violin and would appear now and then. Never enough for him to explain the circumstances. He had a room to himself, what would have been the garage of their house, an extraordinary indulgence, which may have made the kids in the cul-de-sac hate him so much. A large plate-glass window, through the curtains of which you would see the brown head of hair tangled in sheets, not yet awake at the incomprehensible hour of half past ten. He always had money, or knew how to get it, so he was always worth the wait. His absent mother sent him to Belvedere, which cemented the difference, as most of us went to St Paul's Raheny, or Joey's in Marino. But mostly what I remember about him is that he didn't care. Didn't care about the sneers of the other kids, the contempt of their mothers, the admonition of their fathers not to play with him. So we were mostly left alone, as we trundled through adolescence. He had a wicked mouth and no shame about using it, so while the boys avoided us the girls didn't. Fast talking and an olive complexion managed what football never could. And girls were far more interesting, let's face it. Apart from the tedious rituals of courtship, the question am I going out with you, their company was far preferable. Going back and forwards to Belvedere, the walk down O'Connell Street to North Great George's Street afforded him a different kind of company. The kinds who wore their hair in a shocking blonde beehive, like Dusty Springfield. I found a blonde girlfriend myself, who actually worked – she had left school! – and lived on one of those mysterious suburbs on the Southside. Worked in a carpet factory, something to do with the design of the patterns. We would walk across O'Connell Bridge and she would slip a pound note into my hand to pay for the cinema ticket. She would silence my objection by saying, it's 1964, not 1864.

There were clubs, then, and we could fill the whole weekend with them. It is odd, in retrospect, to read accounts of this oppressive, monochrome, grimly celibate culture, and to realize how little of it we experienced. I had a green suede waistcoat, a bomber jacket, lace-up boots with what we then called Cuban heels. I had worked out that from Friday, when school ended, to Monday, when it next began, we could spend almost every waking hour in one club or another. The Green Lounge, up from the College of Surgeons in St Stephen's Green, where the more sophisticated kids swapped purple hearts and you could hear the sounds of English suburban blues bands, Alexis Korner and Manfred Mann. Was it called something else? Or was it the basement of the Green Tureen, in the oven of which Shan Mohangi tried to burn the body of his dismembered girlfriend? Or was it another club in Harcourt Street? I only remember it as the Green Lounge, a few steps down into a basement, where the infra-red lights turned every girl's blouse blue and the speakers boomed with sounds you didn't hear on RTÉ. It opened around midday on Saturday, and would occupy you till the late afternoon. The Go-Go on Sackville Place, the Flamingo, across the road from Wynn's Hotel on Abbey Street. Then there was the more sedate Grove, by the tennis club near Belgrove, where you ended up. All this before you saw Bob Dylan at the Adelphi and everyone in an Aran jumper stood up to leave after his solo set when he brought The Band on stage.

Mucky was older than me, probably by a year. He received another piece of magic from his mother in England, a grant, to Trinity. What Trinity was I had no idea, but the grant came in four times yearly and he would appear at my door with a clutch of pound notes, as if he had robbed some mysterious bank. We would spend his term's grant as quickly as possible, which may have been where the trouble began. He bought an Afghan coat with a furred collar, stacked heels, which made him even taller than he already was. Dope began to make an appearance and something called LSD, and then one summer he vanished. To America, his brother told me, when I knocked expectantly on his window, San Francisco or Los Angeles.

A year passed, until I knocked again. Miami, I was told, he was preaching.

Preaching? I didn't understand. Who preaches? Had he found religion? Joined the priesthood? He had met a bunch of Bible thumpers and found the something his brother called the Lord.

Haiti, I was told, when I knocked again and again I didn't understand. He was a preacher in Haiti.

What was it? A nervous breakdown after an acid trip?

I didn't find out until many years later. My mother was living alone, in the same house. Mucky Dunne had returned, reclaimed the name Kevin and was living somewhere in Raheny. Weightier now, all of the ocelot charm had been taken by the years. But he was married, had two children, worked with one of those revivalist churches Bono might have gone to. Although he didn't come across Bono, working on those soup kitchens at night, doing stints with the Simon Community, working with the homeless. How had this wayward, fatherless kid become this Bible reader? And he was a Bible reader, could quote whole pages of it, he read it with the literal certitude with which he had once read the *Dandy*. Adam and Eve had been untouched by sin in the Garden of Eden, but it was Eve who plucked the apple, Adam who bit it, and Adam's seed was thereafter touched by sin, from Cain and Abel and after Abel's murder by Cain, through Seth and beyond. But Eve, the vessel of the children of Adam, touched by sin, could also be the vessel of those untouched by sin, if such an event were to occur. Hence Mary and the Virgin birth and the good news etc., etc.

Could this be the same kid I had hung around with? There was the same wit, I had to admit to that, the same sense of abandon. If I had proposed that we rob a sweet shop, he would have given it a go. But what had happened?

An aunt of mine died, many years later, and asked my sister to donate money she had left to a charity. It was the time of the earthquake in Haiti and my sister contacted an educational charity there. But she never visited the country. I was heading to the Caribbean and thought I might take a trip there, so gave Mucky another call and asked him what to expect.

He now ran a small mission, he told me, in a village near Cap-Haitien (the far, ungovernable north) and lived in a small tin shack opposite a vodou priest. There was a worship of St Patrick, he told me, under the name Damballa, some transfer-ence of belief that was connected to the snakes that Patrick had, apparently, driven out of Ireland. Which, ironically, meant he was depicted as a snake himself. Also, some deep connec-tion to Guinness.

We were driven into the back country, in 4x4s with armed guards (everyone was armed there, mainly cut-off shotguns, hanging from belts). Through landscapes of unbelievable poverty – but of course whatever deprivation you witness will always be outdone, around the next bend. The donated money had, my sister told me, built two schools. And I was wondering were the schools imaginary, when two breeze-block buildings appeared out of the dusty scrubland. Lines of girls and boys, in immaculate uniforms. Pictures of my aunt, framed, in every classroom. How extraordinary, I thought. She had spent her life as an au pair, or nanny and whatever savings she had managed to gather had built these places. I had to wonder was there a lean-to Pentecostal church in the far north, made of corrugated iron and salvaged wood, with similar pictures of Mucky Dunne?

I wanted to visit the graves of Baron Samedi and Baron Kriminel (graves are important in Haitian vodou as are the mythical barons) and managed to gain admittance to the central graveyard in Port-au-Prince. A lethal place, I was told, for which, once again, armed guards were necessary. So we walked, between guides, with the sawn-off shotguns dangling carelessly from the leather belts, not too dissimilar to the leathers that had long ago swung from the belts of Christian Brothers. We passed the grave of the real Papa Doc who used his black top hat and tails and dark mirrored glasses to mirror the vodou Baron Samedi, the Iwa of the dead. And next to it was the grave of the mythical Baron Samedi himself. Next to it again, the grave of the terrifying and imaginary Baron Kriminel. There were offerings left beneath the graffitied images that could almost have been drawn by Keith Haring or Jean-Michel Basquiat. Or, indeed, by Mucky Dunne, when he was younger. I could find no statues of Damballa. But beneath the graves of Baron Samedi and Baron Kriminel, as Mucky had assured me, were empty Guinness bottles.

The Censorship Index

But Mucky went to fancy-ass Belvedere. His absent mother paid for it. I went to Belgrove, together with the rest of those kids on Baymount Park. We would take a small bus outside of my doorway, called the Littler. And the Führer raised his brilliantined head again. We would sing a song, after crowding into the bus. Hitler won the Littler. Why on earth did this caricature keep appearing, like a pop-up doll? Maybe the ridiculous rhyme. Maybe the 'Colonel Bogey' song we followed it with as the bus pulled off, denigrating the genitalia of the leaders of the Third Reich. Maybe the war movies we described to each other, juddering with imaginary machine-gun fire as we died imaginary deaths. To a primary school then, where the boys were separated from the girls, across a yard that always smelled of urine and sour milk and where I gradually made the unsettling discovery that these teachers were taught by my own father.

I'm not sure I was aware of it at first, performing so badly that I kept my head down in the back row of those wooden desks with the metal leg supports, a little like a Victorian sewing machine. Probably the thirty-third desk, of the forty in the room, which is the only place I remember getting in the only test I can remember. There was the explosion of running before class which the principal, Mr Kelleher, prowled like the dishevelled head chicken in a Beatrix Potter allegory. He had white balding hair, and did resemble some portly barnyard fowl. He had a cane which he rarely used. He kept it hidden in his sleeve and had held it there for so long that the tip had poked a hole in the sleeve of his tweed jacket. Everybody ran in demented circles until he rang a metal bell and we all lined up and were marched inside. Very little beating, as far as I remember, an hour or so of exquisite boredom until the bell rang again and we ran outside and continued to trace those demented circles. We were city boys and every teacher was, for some strange reason, from the country. Except for one rather handsome youngish man from somewhere on the Southside who took exception to some behaviour of mine and slapped me across the face. I must have deserved it. But it wasn't a farmer's hand. He had long manicured nails, as I remember it, and one of them drew blood. A tiny cut across my left cheek, and a telltale streak of red.

His concern was extraordinary. He took out a handkerchief, dabbed the affected wound. Told me to hold it, brought me to an isolated desk near the front, and even gave me a boiled sweet to calm my nerves. I didn't know what nerves were, but when the class day ended and he checked the wound, wiped it clear of whatever dried blood had congealed, I finally understood. My father was his '*cigire*'. His school inspector. His lecturer in St Patrick's College, Drumcondra, and among his duties was the supervision of the graduates. One of whom had the added burden of teaching me.

It was a strange destiny and was to follow me for years. There were three routes to secure employment in that arid Dublin of the fifties: the civil service, the banks or the teaching profession. Most of the country, it seemed, chose the latter. I would hear the refrain constantly. Your father taught me. Whoever teaches teachers? These giants who prowled the paths between our darkwood desks needed teaching themselves? He had lectured them, on the leafy campus on Drumcondra Road, next to the Archbishop's Palace. He had sent them into the unlettered populace of this new republic (only finally proclaimed, after all, in 1949) with a mission to educate. 'Educere', he would tell them, from the Latin, which means to lead out. I would later learn there was another Latin root, 'educare', which means something like the opposite: to stuff in. But leading out or stuffing in had no effect on me, his eldest son. I was, as John McGahern would sardonically inform him, the living contradiction of all of his educational theories.

Mr McGahern replaced the handsome Dubliner with the manicured fingernails. He had a country accent, like most graduates of St Pat's and my father was inevitably his *cigire*, supervisor. School inspector. His nickname, I would learn later, was 'Cliffy'. My father's, not Mr McGahern's, who didn't stay long enough with us to acquire a nickname. Cliffy, because of the way he pronounced the Irish word for games. *Cluiche*, with the West of Ireland inflection which made an 'f' of the otherwise soft 'ch'.

McGahern also wore a brown tweed suit and the only memory I have of him is of him leaning out of the open window, skinny in that brown tweed suit, picking his nose. He seemed to have things to think about, other than the forty boys who shivered behind him and wished he'd close that window. Then one day he vanished.

I suppose a disappearing act should never be given an explanation. The magician should always keep the trick mysterious. The beauty in the short skirt and the top hat vanishes in a puff of smoke. How did he do it? Where did she go? Then abracadabra and the smoke billows and she appears again.

Mr McGahern never appeared again. Vanished from our lives as if he'd never existed. There was not a word of explanation, from the principal, the parents, from the next graduate of my father's who replaced him. And I suppose our question was, who was the magician, where did this magic come from? And why?

It was from the source of all miracles, where all magic comes from. A book. John McGahern was a writer, one of the best in the latter half of the twentieth century. He had, around the time he appeared in our classroom, published a book. The book had been banned, as most books were, and yet he continued to teach. I befriended him later in life when I began to publish books myself, although friend was probably a relative term with John. He had that subversive country habit of turning gossip into a wicked anecdote. Charlie Haughey, he told me once, was walking down Grafton Street with Albert Reynolds (both would become Taoiseach – prime minister – of Ireland). He points across the street to two young girls, walking in the opposite direction. You see those ladies? I'm going to marry one of them. Which, asks Albert? It doesn't matter, Charlie replies, They're both the Taoiseach's daughters.

John wrote a book later in life that explained his vanishing act. He called it *The Leavetaking*. He hid very little in this barely fictional account, not even the name of my father. The magician in question was not the school principal, the bumbling Mr Kelleher, but the school patron, the equally Dickensian and portly Father Cartan. The book described with uncanny exactitude the atmosphere of the schoolyard, the frayed elbow of Mr Kelleher's coat with the cane sticking out and added details I could never have been aware of, but might have suspected. The seagulls, picking at the discarded lunch sandwiches in the concrete yard. The slightly green coloured steps of the urinals behind. The benign chaos of Mr Kelleher's own house, where the discipline he maintained within Belgrove's walls was totally absent. And John's fault was not, apparently, publishing a banned book, but marrying a Scandinavian divorcee.

I suppose publishing a book is, on the level of moral infractions, an expected one. Every writer seemed to have been a teacher once, even Joyce for God's sake, and the litany of those who taught or were banned would go on forever. Frank O'Connor, Brendan Behan, Edna O'Brien. But marrying a Scandinavian divorcee crossed a different Rubicon. Blonde hair, with a helmet-cut bob, straight out of a Bergman movie like *Summer with Monika*, not only Scandinavian but married once, maybe twice, God forgive us how many times before?

The Leavetaking is hardly a comedy, but, given the genius of the detached perspective, could almost be one. And it had my father on the fringes of the action, so I had to ask him about it.

He had retired by then, having had his own battles with the unseen forces that seemed to govern Irish life. A new department of education had been opened in University College Dublin and he was the natural – maybe the only – candidate for the professorship. I remember when he did me the honour of asking me should he apply, and the odd sense of privilege I felt in even being asked that question. I insisted he should, because if he didn't, a cleric would take it. He thought about it, and then demurred. Because he probably already knew a cleric would in fact take it. And a cleric did take it, the bursar of the college he had taught teachers in for years, a man with no educational qualifications whatsoever.

So I had to ask him about John's account, of his Belgrove vanishing act, and he told me a strange story, which, being John's supervisor, he would know.

The principal, Mr Kelleher, didn't want any trouble. The National Teachers' Union, even less. To remove a teacher from his or her post would require something like an act of parliament. Even the bumbling parish priest, the 'patron' of the school, wanted no fuss. But the parents of that secure middle-class burgh, Clontarf, came together and marched to the parish priest's house, demanding John's removal.

I could never be sure what the lesson was here. One lived in a priest-ridden society, it was obvious. Schools, hospitals, orphanages, even universities were run by religious orders. Passing a church on the 30 bus, whole rows of passengers would bless themselves. As Samuel Beckett said, even the dogs will someday do it. So when in the eighties, after a sea of referendums, the whole edifice of Catholicism collapsed, I couldn't quite believe in the delirium. Surely half of the society – in fact maybe much more than half – must have been complicit with the church. It's hard to forget a suburb in which, on the day after Pancake Tuesday (was it always a Tuesday?) every single passerby wore a smear of ash on their forehead. Equally hard to dispel the image of the good parishioners of Clontarf queuing up outside the parish priest's house (it was next to St Gabriel's Church, across from Cronin's the chemist) to demand the expulsion of this absent-minded genius who had the temerity to teach their children.

I often wonder what would have happened had the *cigire* applied for that university job. He retired, asked me for money to help him and my mother buy the caravan near Mornington, the place where she was born. I had begun to write and make films by then and was happy to do so.

I used to compare myself to rock and roll stars who buy their parents mansions. I bought mine a caravan.

He knew, I suppose, that the departments of philosophy, sociology and the soon-to-be department of education would all be under the patronage of the Archbishop's Palace, next door. Maybe he was tired of it all. Maybe his eclecticism was too suspect. The chair in education was given to an accountant and a priest. The inevitable wade through a clerical swamp would hardly have been worth it. But maybe he would have lived longer. He died soon after, four or five years, in the mudflats of the Nanny river

I was in Los Angeles when I got the news. *The Company of Wolves* was showing at a festival. Oddly enough, of all I had written and made, it probably would have satisfied him the most. When I got back to the hotel there was a telegram waiting. Call home.

On the long flight back I wondered how he would haunt me. He always told ghost stories, so it was the least that could be expected of him. Headless horsemen, charging down a country road, during the night of the Cleggan Bay Disaster. A gentleman in an undertaker's hat, who he meets in the grounds of St

Anne's Estate. Who tells him the day is for the living, the night is for the dead. The ghosts were always from some decades back, from his father's generation. They wore long cloaks, top hats, squeaky boots. They could have strolled out of the doors of Marino Crescent, where Bram Stoker once lived. Next to the Fairview Cinema, where all the film versions of his *Dracula* once played. But maybe the real ghost was the smiling peasant outside the thatched cottage with the squeezebox in his hand.

Fictions

One of the first stories I wrote was called *Night in Tunisia*
after the Dizzy Gillespie tune and was set in the same,
inevitable Bettystown up from that Nanny river. All of the
details are true. The endless sand blowing across the dunes,
the sound of the rain on the corrugated rooftops, the sound of
the thuck of a tennis ball whacked across the net. But none of
the characters are. I invented a father, who was a saxophone
player in the declining world of showbands. A son, who had
some musical talent but didn't want to exercise it. Maybe the
invention was necessary. Maybe it releases some inner voice,
allows one to say what couldn't otherwise be spoken. But the
reality was quite different.

He played the violin. Quite well, actually. He played jigs and
reels he might have learned from his own father's squeezebox,
but really came into his own with the classical repertoire. I
was forced into violin lessons, which I hated, then to classical guitar lessons, which I loved. We would play Bach pieces
together occasionally, him on the violin, me transposing the
cello parts for the guitar. 'Jesu, Joy of Man's Desiring'. But the
real adventure was the weekly visit to the St Francis Xavier

Sketch by Eithne Jordan.

Hall, in Sherrard Street, where the RTÉ National Symphony Orchestra played their concerts.

The enticement would be quite subtle. An embossed invitation – maybe they were tickets, that he had paid for, maybe he had some other kind of subscription – would be left on the mantelpiece above the fireplace in the sitting room. There was a low-slung armchair beneath it, next to the record player which I would use to help me read whatever piece I was working on. Julian Bream, or John Williams, playing the same old Bach, or Granados or Villa-Lobos or the transcendent Francisco Tárrega. I learned very early that practice was a way of avoiding housework, so while my sisters laboured with the dishes in the kitchen,

I worked on the intricacies of Bach's Partita in D Minor. I never quite mastered that one, but managed to never wash a dish.

The invitation would sit there on the mantelpiece for a day or two, and one of us would enquire as to what was playing this week, Beethoven, Schumann, Stravinsky, Berlioz, and express an interest in going. I generally took it up. What age would I have been? Eleven, twelve? And we would troop off, in the bus, or did we have a car then? Again, I can't remember. But I remember the hall. The sound of the orchestra tuning up. The semi-circular fan of the players. The sense of emotional expectation. The entry of the conductor. Tibor Paul was his name, with a mysterious Magyar ring to it. (He was actually from Budapest.) Why Tibor Paul? Why not Paul Tibor? It belonged to a realm where the names were different, where the sense of a musical event had a moral, almost sacred aura. The long dark tails the man wore, the raising of the baton, the absolute and immediate silence. And then the strange confusion after each caesura of sound, when it stopped, however briefly. Is this when you clap? No. Can we cough now? Perhaps. The explosion of applause when the proper movement ended. How did they know? And who was that strange gentleman, his hands full of manuscripts, in the front row?

It could have been Frederick May, whose family owned May's music store where you bought your sheet music. It could have been Charles Acton, the overweight and always formally dressed music critic for the *Irish Times*. The manuscript was the score, of course. Only those truly in the know could read one, could even get one. There was a strange displacement to the whole experience. It felt foreign and immediately familiar, all at once. Foreign, because of the strange theatricality of the experience. Familiar because of the emotions it evoked. You felt you already knew that melody from Berlioz, Mozart, Saint-Saëns.

But Dublin was a stranger country then. Modernity had hardly touched it. If I was twelve at those concerts it would have been 1962. The hall was still the St Francis Xavier Hall, a name as foreign to me as the Mathew of the Father Mathew Hall, where the Father Mathew Feis Ceoil was held, a set of musical competitions for aspiring violinists, cellists, and classical guitarists, like me. The Francis Saviour would later become the SFX where U2 would introduce themselves to the world. The letters SFX cannily disguised its origins but had more connection to the founder of the Jesuits than U2 did to the Lockheed Martin spy plane. It was a different world and it's odd to miss it. I don't miss the cavernous churches, the loudspeakers hanging from each lamp post on Holy Week, but I miss the city that had hardly changed since 1906, the mixture of high culture and low behaviour, the Grafton Street where every second shop seemed to be a bookshop. The joke about the Irish navvy who was asked the difference between a joist and a girder. Well, that Joyce, he wrote *Ulysses*, didn't he? And didn't that Goethe write *Faust*?

It was all about to change, anyway. I bought my father a record for his birthday, a version of 'Moon River' by Danny Williams. Not the white Williams, Andy. Danny, with the voice like a dark angel that seemed to be the harbinger of Sam Cooke. He said, you bought this for yourself, didn't you? And I had to admit I did. But I thought he might listen to it.

He didn't.

I stopped going to the concerts after that. The embossed invitations would turn up on the mantelpiece and I never lifted them again. Did he go alone? I don't know. But each week another would appear, saying more than a spoken word could. Please come, they seemed to say. Let things be as they were. There was a certain cruelty, maybe, in never taking the bait. But maybe I was simply doing what kids do. Growing up. Bob Dylan would soon be playing in the Carlton. The Francis Xavier would become the SFX.

Would that have made a better story than the saxophone player in the summer hut with the tin roof and his reluctantly musical son? I don't know. It would be missing that wonderful sound, of rain on the corrugated iron roof.

The real question is why I had to disguise the reality to write about it. Maybe that's why it's called fiction. And now I've got to tell it twice.

Sex

It began with birdwatching. I was obsessive about birds, their nests, and unfortunately for a while, their eggs. The old overgrown Guinness estate they called St Anne's was an unstructured sanctuary for them and I would spend hours ferreting out the nest of a wren, a starling, a ring ouzel, a blackbird, a thrush, climb a tree to a sparrow hawk's nest, or run – for some reason we always ran – over to Dollymount Strand and the long grasses among the dunes and follow the path of a skylark to its nest, or a mallard and once even a swan. The theory was that if you didn't disturb the nest, took just one egg out of many, the clutch would survive. And then it was made known to me that this was just a theory, so the habit of collecting those delicate blue or white or brown and speckled eggs, piercing both ends with a pin and blowing the yolk out with your lips or with a piece of hollow straw had to be replaced by something else. In my case it was binoculars, and friends of mine who had no interests in the habits of the lesser crested grebe began to take an interest.

Can I borrow them?

No.

I'll come with you then. We'll both play.

What's the game?

Spying.

So spying it was, in the long grass. Following a young man, or a young woman with the double lenses through the bushes or trees, generally to a secluded area where one would meet the other or where both would imagine they were unobserved.

What are we looking for?

For him to take her clothes off.

Aha.

But he rarely did. We would see them, an arm around a shoulder, perhaps, a meeting of heads, a gentle or a tossing movement of the head, and then a slow descent into the long grass around them.

We have to get closer.

Again, why?

Because they're going to start it soon.

Start what?

Riding.

What is riding?

Riding, he told me, was where he puts his thing into her and they go hopping along.

His thing into her? I knew something happened in that area. But hopping along? I could barely imagine it.

But we squirmed closer, through our own long grasses. Like Gregory Peck in *The Guns of Navarone*, the target being the dim outline of that couple, viewed through the binocular lens. And there did seem to be some movement, of the grass itself, or the bodies behind it, but it wasn't a movement that I, at least, would define as hopping. It was slow and languorous and twisted back and forth, moving the long curtain of grass with it. Until suddenly a head rises up, looks towards us, over the flowering heads of the grass, which seemed to be moving in slow motion. Is it the man? No, it's the girl. Long brown hair, pulled back. Holding a blouse to her chest. Then after her, the man, pulling his trousers on, running, like a lethal German stormtrooper, towards us.

We ran then, faster than him. And he returned to his version of hopping.

So this was the subject of sex, which makes a fantasist out of everyone. How were the *Kinsey Reports* ever written, on this strange, shifting substratum to our daily lives, about which nobody ever tells the truth. Then again, Kinsey said nothing about hopping.

There was a girl called Roisin Sex who lived in Furry Park. Forgive me, Roisin, for remembering your name, you had probably no idea of the effect it had on Belgrove boys.

There were very few furs in Furry Park and the Sexes might have had little to do with sex, although I imagine Roisin must have been cursed by that surname. She had brown hair, as far as I remember, and had a fuller bosom earlier than most, brown eyes with a kind of Jewish look to them. I used to think because of the name and those eyes that the family came from the furthest reaches of Eastern Europe. A corruption of Sax, maybe? There was an Adolphe Sax who combined the clarinet and the trumpet into something called the saxophone and maybe that gave the name its reason. But, no, I discovered later, the surname had a sound Anglo-Saxon origin, like the word itself, from the fens of medieval England. So sex, like most questionable things, came from across the water.

I know the more adventurous boys used to chase Roisin, hoping to get her into the long grass behind the schoolyard where everything her family name implied could be explored, but she was far more sensible than them. She seemed unembarrassed by the name and anyway preferred the company of girls.

As did I. Girls were more interesting, had more fun, didn't talk all day about soccer and didn't want to punch you in the mouth. They also gave rise to a strange erotic swirl, a heady desire to know more, of them and everything about them. Nothing to do with sex, and its foreign implications. No, it was more mysterious than that, the meeting of eyes across a privet hedge, the intertwining of hands, a group of them, heads clustered together like daisies, one of them nodding towards you, across Vernon Avenue. You fell in and out of friendships like a wandering pod, blown by the wind into some girl's hair. But there was something else going on, something to do with the absent emperor observing you in that bed of nettles. You could become someone else through another's gaze, be those eyes brown, grey or blue.

The first eyes were almost almond shaped and coloured and she lived with her mother who ran the sweet shop near where Vernon Avenue turned into Conquer Hill Road. It wasn't really a shop, just a small, delightful bungalow behind the inevitable privet hedge, the front door of which had been cut in half, like a western bar room. Brown tiles on the roof, lace curtains on the single window, a small cement path leading from the metal gate to the half-open wooden door. Her mother would dole out choc ices and Maltesers from behind this half-door to the queue of boys and girls coming back from school. She had an oriental look, dark page-boy hair and dark brown eyes, which was perfected in the sweet miniature of her daughter. There seemed to be no father, which was an immense relief, and your first implication that you were the favoured one came when the mother opened the bottom half of the door and invited you inside. There were treats to be had, more than your few pennies could afford, and there was the delicious sense of being let linger on, until her daughter came from the dark interior, having divested herself of that blue and grey school uniform into a summer skirt and a yellow cardigan. Small shoes, slippers, really. If anyone looked more like Anna May Wong in *Shanghai Express*, both mother and daughter, I have yet to meet them. She went with you, tolerated you, walked with you across the Bull Bridge sleepers hand in hand, even kissed you in the long grasses of the dunes on Dollymount Strand. This kiss was called a 'wear' for some reason, a word that bore as little resemblance to the meeting of lips as the word 'riding' did to the sexual business. You could wear without riding, but could you ride without wearing? It would remain a mystery for some time.

These affections, though, would change with the seasons, the erotic charge would move on, from you or from her, and you were once again like that wandering dandelion pod, looking for a new girl's blowing hair with which you could tangle. You would stick there for a while until the next wind blew you on again. Other boyfriends were the only problem, the ones she left you for or the ones she left for you. You weren't good at fisticuffs in either case. The throb of a motorbike behind you down Vernon Avenue always meant trouble. Males in general were to be avoided. Females, much better.

You never knew how it began; you were chosen again and another hand would be slipping into yours, walking across

O'Connell Bridge, now to the cinema, this hand contained a pound note, for the pictures. Clint Eastwood, in that western where they insulted his mule, and he shot the whole street up. I can't take this, you would say, but she worked, had left school, was older than you, had a job in a carpet factory. And it mightn't have been the sex, the promise of eroticism, it might have been the movies themselves, The Man With No Name, Oddjob in *Goldfinger* with his lethal bowler hat and the golden girl on the bed, naked and dead. Someone had to pay for the cinema, the popcorn during and the ice-cream after and whatever happened in between. Her brother would drive her from the Southside to the Northside to the tennis hut called the Grove and pick her up after the dance had ended and whatever passion between you had exhausted itself, by another privet hedge, under a streetlamp that always seemed to have a halo of mist around it.

Did they all merge into one? The same school uniform, only the colour changing, from Holy Faith to Manor House to Santa Sabina, out by the more sophisticated Sutton. One uniform was blue, the other grey, the other with blue and grey stripes. The after-school garb was better: socks, always pushed down for some reason over shoes with a bit of a heel. A pleated skirt and a cardigan, bunched up to the elbows. And the lure might not have been sex after all. Just company.

My Paedophile

In fact, my most enduring relationship from those years was with a paedophile. I could call him my paedophile. The girls came and went, but he stayed. Persisted, even. Maybe he wanted to be Batman to my Robin. Or the Lone Ranger to my Tonto. Or Zeus to my Ganymede. The latter was more likely, although I doubt he was familiar with the mythological reference. But, like Zeus, he would speak from the shadows, or like the Jewish god Jahweh from behind a bush. There was no horse called Silver either, but a bicycle on which I'd be cycling lazily to school, both elbows perched on the handlebars, and from the bush, or from one of the dark trunks of those evergreen oaks, would come the voice.

Ne-el.

At first I thought it might be the squeak of my front wheel, or the wind in those dark green, buttony leaves. I would cycle on, but a day or two later hear the same celestial voice again.

Ne-el.

And now a figure would reveal itself, darting from tree to tree. A long gaberdine coat, something like the one Buster Keaton wore in the Samuel Beckett film called, simply, *Film*.

He would manage to keep pace with me, and even begin a conversation, always from among the cover of those evergreen oaks. His interest, apparently, was not in me, but in my sister.

Your sister Ursula is very saxy, Ne-el.

Saxy. He meant sex. Maybe that was his name as well. I would never learn it. But he knew mine.

I was being watched, she was being watched.

I don't know what I replied. Did I agree? She was? But his interest, I sensed already, was not in her. I had to admire the sleight of hand of the erotic transference. He had this cunning ability to get into the most unlikely places without me quite realizing how he got there. A bit, again, like a magician performing a trick that you knew was a trick, with the mechanism ingeniously hidden. He finagled himself onto the bar of my bike – or did he place me on the bike, and offer to cycle me home? I can't quite remember, but I do remember this skinny form close to mine, the squeak of the bicycle wheels, the unwashed gaberdine coat, the tobaccoey breath, as he waxed lyrical about her charms. Very saxy.

I had to agree. She was turning into a woman of undoubted qualities, already with a slew of suitors.

Could you get me to meet her, Ne-el?

I doubted I could. They were all square-jawed, athletic types. One of them apparently owned a hotel in Bray. Drove all the way over to Dollymount to see her in a Jaguar car.

Did I tell him all this? I hope I did. But it would have been to no effect anyway, as his interest in the 'saxy' way she walked was entirely feigned. He was interested in me. He left me at the corner of the Gaelic pitch on Mount Prospect

Avenue. There was a reason, I was sure. He didn't want to venture too close to home. He knew my name, and knew where I lived.

Of course he did, because he'd seen you before. And maybe the emperor was there too, watching him, watching you. This dreaded self-awareness, when did it begin? But once it visited, it would never leave. Now you're swimming by the curved china-blue shelter on the Bull Wall, looking out on the yellow gantries of the docks and that awkward moment comes when you have to wrap the towel round yourself to get the togs on, or, even worse, off, and you could stand naked for the briefest moment with your friends in the suddenly cold wind but there's somebody watching, in the shadow of the cement roof. How long has he been watching? You don't know. He is a creature of Dollymount Strand, St Anne's Estate, the empty unpoliced spaces, the promise of the tall grass where couples would engage in that business you weren't yet sure of. Something to do with generation. Riding, one of your birdwatching friends had told you. You had tired of the pursuit and rented out your binoculars to others who wanted to use them for purposes other than birdwatching. But by now you know there is very little hopping involved.

You wonder about this riding business while waiting for yet another girlfriend by the Pillar. Have you enough money to play the cinematic jukebox in Funland? You also wonder about that tautological sign: Come In And Have Fun In Funland. You knew more about words than about adult activities like riding. Tautology, you knew, was something about using the same word twice. Then another dapper gent approaches from behind. Would you like a cigarette? Is he the same one? Is he the watcher? This one doesn't have a cigarette case, but a pack of Sweet Aftons. No, you won't have one. Because you can see the girl getting off the bus on the Carlton side of O'Connell Street and you cross the busy street to meet her, in through the glass doors of Funland and you wish you had taken that cigarette to signify your adulthood as you slide your few pennies into the cinematic jukebox and see Billy Fury singing 'Halfway to Paradise'. You wonder will he be waiting, outside the Pillar turnstile when you emerge, but he won't, because he is only the harbinger to your paedophile. The John the Baptist to his Jesus Christ.

Because my paedophile was not one of those who hung around the Pillar, nor was he one of those priests who prowled between the desks, beat the most vulnerable pretty ones until they cried, then perched them on his knee to comfort them. My paedophile didn't smoke cigarettes, didn't teach in the school, seemed nervous when the playing fields came into view, inhabited the thicker parts of the woods in St Anne's Estate as if he belonged to the tangled undergrowth and the green moss that came off the bark of the sycamore trees. He was a green, polleny creature and seemed to come from the forests deep inside. There were forests inside you could get lost in as surely as the ones outside

What extraordinary persistence, you come to think. There is a dedication here that is superhuman, maybe even supernatural. He seems to know your movements better than yourself. We'd be swimming by the Bull Wall, framed by the gantries of the North Wall, next to the tiny cottages of the East Wall. Why were there so many walls? Something to do with the buttressing of the city beyond against the tides. I can

see myself as he would have seen me, hulking in the corner of
the cement shelter, watching me, Brian Crowley and probably
Dicky Leech as we did the awkward business with the towels
and the wet togs and the summer pants and T-shirt lying on
the wet steps. Wasn't there someone there, in the shadow of
the curved cement shelter. No, it couldn't have been my paedophile. It was a cloud passing over the sun.

Neither was my paedophile the one who raped the next-
door neighbour whom your father found in the wilder reaches
of the park. This one was a boy, not a girl. Raped by someone
else's paedophile and you're not sure what it even means, rape,
how it can be enacted on a boy and not a girl, but you know
it's something to do with the culmination of the general wave
of violence that seems to come and go in that place, like the
weather. Your father gives what succour he can to the boy, calls
the police and is eventually called to give evidence when the
case comes to court. The assailant, being a junior from a gang
you know across the park, gets a term in whatever borstal
deals with crimes like that. But the term is short, less than six
months, and he's eventually released. He meets your friends
in the more tangled innards of the park, beyond the rotting
ornamental lake and swears revenge for the evidence that put
him inside. Revenge, not on the father, but on the son. So he
threatens to make himself your own very personal paedophile.
You avoid the park then, for as long as you can, finding it hard
to imagine even the idea of such revenge. Until a car, a Mini,
is robbed on the Oscar Traynor Road, which goes all the way
from Killester through Kilbarrack on to Sutton Cross. There
is a boy in your class in Belgrove called Oscar Traynor and
you wonder how he got a road named after him. Something

to do with 1916, you are told, but you can't connect this red-lipped, angelic kid with gunfire and explosions any more than you can connect your next-door neighbour with the idea of rape, or with the car thief, being chased by a squad car, from Killester through Raheny to Kilbarrack who crashes into a lamp post somewhere near Sutton Cross. Dies instantly. The thief happens to be the rapist and your relief is immediate and complicated. How can you be happy that another kid died? Even if he threatened you with rape, a concept you are only beginning to get a handle on? Died like James Dean in *Rebel Without a Cause*, in a game of chicken with a police car? But life, you are beginning to realize, is complicated. This savage garden of a park is complicated.

But it's yours now, to wander in again, where your very own paedophile is waiting. Any long acquaintance breeds familiarity. He sits on a wall, between the football pitch and the road, and the other kids, tired of football, begin burning matches from behind, setting his hair alight. It doesn't burn very well, being everything you would imagine a paedophile's hair to be, thin and altogether wispy. He imagines a midge or a bluebottle is nibbling at his ears and flicks it away, to a ripple of laughter that he doesn't understand. When they light it again and it flares from the back, in a sudden scald that almost melts his skin, he cries out, in a piteous, powerless howl. And you feel that most confusing thing, then, pity, for this shadow that has been following you since you were old enough to take the 30 bus. He scurries towards that bus now, leaving the odour of singed hair and the sound of laughter.

Why pity? Because they laughed at him. Because he could feel pain, like anybody else. If you prick them, do they not bleed? If you burn them, do they not blister? Because he's your paedophile, not anybody else's.

You're free of him in the clubs, and in the cinema. Because he would look absurd under the infra-red bulbs, those strange teeth shining blue like your girlfriend's bra, showing under the white blouse. Because he's too old for clubs. Because he doesn't like the cinema. Too much of him on the screen, as Dracula bends his teeth down to Mimi. You walk down Fairview Park, past the crumbling eighteenth-century crescent on Malahide Road where the inventor of Dracula lived. That's free of him, too. Maybe he doesn't like vampires. St Anne's is his park, not Fairview.

But then, sitting on the same 30 bus, coming home at night, you're older now and there he is, behind you. The same voice in your ear. Ne-el. He gains courage and rises, shifts into your seat. He looks different. He has either oiled his hair back or is wearing a toupee. There is no longer that mushroomy smell, of rotting wood and mulch. You feel his knee against yours. I just came back from England, Ne-el, and the laws are different over there for the boys round Piccadilly. The conversation has advanced now, it seems, your sister is no longer part of the pretence and you wonder how you will get rid of him this time. You haven't got the language really, to counter it or to make your escape. But a next-door neighbour sitting down the bus, a kindly woman, attractive, too, with brown hair who could have been your Venus if you wanted one instead of a paedophile, she seems to know what's going on. Sees a youth, fourteen or fifteen, hemmed in by an older gent in one of those gaberdine raincoats. She moves to the front of the bus, says hello Neil, and she pronounces your name correctly and the relief is enormous, I think our stop is coming up.

She gets you to walk her home, down Baymount Park, a few houses from the back garden of your own. She has brown hair, a sympathetic face and you walk arm in arm, all grown up now and you wonder will she invite you in and how you would deal with all of the resultant complications. But you have another girlfriend now, a brown-haired one who dumped her boyfriend to pursue you. You didn't want her to dump this boyfriend; he drove a motorbike and dressed like a rocker, while you dressed like a mod. But maybe that was the attraction, she wanted to move from rockers to mods. You have heard the thrum of his motorbike as he follows you both on the long walk home. But at least that sound is better than the rustle of your paedophile. So you let this motherly Venus kiss you on the cheek and walk past the long privet hedge of your back garden, where the 30 bus is departing now, in a brown cloud of exhaust and you walk through it into the front garden and there he is, in the shadow of the privet hedge.

He offers you money. What's the money for? You ask. You know. Says again he's come back from London where Irish boys can make a lot of money that way. You say no thanks and make your way back inside.

And you wonder why it has persisted, this pursuit. Are you his only Ganymede? If so, what devotion, from the age of ten to this. The girlfriends come and go, but is he to be the only consistent one? Like tea leaves, always at the bottom of the cup. You wonder where he lives, when he seeks you out, does he wake up one day and say, I must check out that Ne-el again, find out what he is doing. Or has he been always looking, waiting for the right moment to intervene?

What patience, though. Every now and then, outside the college you attended, waiting for another bus, the 46A or B, on the Southside now, you hear it. Ne-el. Did somebody say that or did I imagine it, or could that really be him again, cycling by in the gaberdine coat?

The League for a
Workers' Republic

You went to university, the priorities were changing, everything was politics now, republican clubs and the Communist Party of Ireland or the Irish Communist Party. They were different apparently, one was more internationalist than the other. Ho Ho Chi Minh, the NLF are going to win. You had no interest in politics, but all the glamorous people did. Boys with long military coats and Che Guevara beards and moustaches selling pamphlets on the steps up to the big metal doors

Interesting to read Marx in the long hall of Earlsfort Terrace library, but you wondered why the political stars were always the pretty ones. I was in Paris last year, '68, I witnessed first-hand, etc. You weren't in Paris, couldn't conceive of it. There were huge meetings in the Aula Max, a diminutive poet from Scotland turned up to speak and no one knew who he was, but you did, you had read *A Drunk Man Looks at the Thistle*. And then summer came and you went to London. You could conceive of London.

A friend of yours was a nice middle-class girl from Clontarf, studying German. She was a friend of another friend, quite a shy girl until she sat by the piano and played it like a demon. Khachaturian's 'Sabre Dance'. This friend had a boyfriend who was an electrician, Peter Graham, a member either of the Irish Workers' Group (Marxist–Leninist) or the League for a Workers' Republic, whichever of them supported the Official IRA in the North. Either one, it didn't matter to you.

Peter had a genuine moustache, an electrician's moustache, not a UCD revolutionary's one; he was small, alert and wiry and you liked him. All that you wondered was why? Why him and this rather prim, middle-class girl from the better end of Clontarf, with the blonde page-boy hair that could have been worn by one of your maiden aunts? They're heading to London, a couple, apparently, and ask you to go with them. You're chosen to go over there in advance, pool whatever money you could raise and find a flat.

You take the boat and the train, and end up on the Green in front of Euston Station, and go about the business of finding an affordable flat.

But it's the height of summer, everywhere is busy, every-where, it seems, is taken. You stay in a B&B for a night or two, and then find out that you have run out of money. You go to Euston Station to meet the train from Holyhead each day, more impoverished than the day before, but they never turn up. You need somewhere to sleep and, as it's the height of summer, Euston Green seems as comfortable as any other option (the others would be Hyde Park, Green Park and the tiny little park in Soho Square.)

So there you are, sleeping on Euston Green and waiting for Peter Graham and the student of German to turn up. You can barely remember how you became the advance guard for them and their revolution but most of the money is gone and while the sun shines on the Green around Euston Station the grass is kind of filthy and soon you become filthy, too. There was an underworld of rough sleepers that you become part of without really knowing how or why. So you grow acquainted with the public toilets that had showers in them, soup kitchens and the various scams that keep you alive and fed while nothing else is working. There's a kind of job you can get, not really a job, more of a stipend, to keep you fed while wandering. Becoming a walking advertisement, carrying a sandwich board which you pick up in an office somewhere around King's Cross. The deal seems to be, you line up, sign some kind of paper and take your allotted sandwich board for the day, to amble the streets around Green Park, Euston Station, down to the river and back. The insider's advice is that it's money for nothing, you collect the board, walk a few streets and then plonk yourself in some adjacent park for the day. Which you do. The board they give you, who can no longer afford a flat, let alone a down payment, is advertising a flat rental service and reads: 2000 FLATS. You're too tired and hungry to enjoy the irony. So you collect your board, made your way to the nearest shaded park and do your best to sleep. But on returning the sandwich board, about seven hours later, you're docked the promised payment. You haven't been walking, you're told. So they have spies out and the street walking is obligatory.

You can lean the sandwich board, though, advertising 2000 flats, against a red phone box and use whatever pennies you had left to call the various advertised numbers, looking for a flat to rent. You can even walk the sandwich board to different addresses, all of which are already taken. Useless to ring the number on the sandwich board you're carrying, since they demand two weeks' deposit, and the money is already running out.

The League for the
Sex Workers' Republic

You were walking down Oxford Street wearing the sand-wich board advertising 2000 flats and wondering where you would sleep that night. The payment received as a walking advertisement barely paid for food. The square on Euston Green was getting rough, fires burning there at night, down and outs even filthier than you drinking cheap sherry until the cops came to disperse them, which made sleeping there an even dodgier proposition. You wondered should you call home, but calls across the water were expensive and, besides, you could feel the blush, underneath the grime on your face, of something you recognized as shame. You wondered did your father ever carry a sandwich board advertising 2000 flats while waiting for two revolutionaries to arrive at Euston Station. Maybe your grandfather did. But revolutions would have been different then.

If you could make it through another night, your promised partners might turn up. You passed a three-card trick act on the pavement: one of them swirled the cards, find the lady, while the other two pretended to put down the money. It was probably the fifth time that day you passed them, come on, Pat, try your luck, they went to pull you towards the three-card table, and you shook your head, did you look like you had any money? You walked on and heard a whistle, they waved something in the air, your passport. They had picked your pocket under a sandwich board. You had to admire their dexterity, and then their generosity as they found it quite empty of notes and tossed it back. Honour among thieves. Mind how you go.

So you'd deposit the sandwich board back at the King's Cross office, take whatever payment would feed you for the evening and you must have been standing on the King's Cross platform, when the couple spied you, dressed in the regulation outfits of hippies those days – some kind of Afghan sheepskin bursting out around the sleeves and collar, tangled reddish hair.

You look lost, head.

Being addressed as a human softens something.

You admitted you were, a little.

We have a friend who has a crash pad, if you want a bed for the evening.

The term 'crash pad' is comforting, as is the Scottish accent. You wondered what you had done to deserve such kindness.

So all three of you get on the Northern line. You saw the backs of those Victorian stucco houses pass by the Tube window. You tried to picture the promised crash pad. A dusty rug over bare floorboards. High ceiling, high windows. The kinds of conversations you were never quite able for, about red leb and acid. You never smoked dope, took drugs. But maybe you could sleep, under the smell of hashish and patchouli oil, while Canned Heat played on the turntable.

Those tall Victorian houses, with the expansive tattered gardens, were gradually replaced by a meaner kind of dwelling. The Tube went way beyond Central London, Notting Hill and Ladbroke Grove, and the realm of squats and crash pads, if they had ever existed. The Scottish couple said little, smiled at you every now and then with an implicit understanding that seemed to say not long now.

You got out at the end of the line, and moved through endless streets of the kinds of house you had grown up in, a small, cramped garden, maybe a car in the driveway, the lace curtains of the living room lit by a flickering television. You wondered what kind of commune could have established itself here, but it was a new world and you had to trust those Afghan sheepskins that were leading the way.

A gate creaked open then, and they walked up to one doorway, indistinguishable from a thousand others. A doorbell rang, and the door was opening by an imposing, rather fat Turkish or Levantine man in a suit. He greeted the couple and they led you inside. You could glimpse the kind of interior where the new-bought sofa is still covered in its plastic wrapping. Hang on, you thought, and remembered why you had always hated hippies, and turned to question them, but they were already gone.

How extraordinary, you think. You've been sold. And you could only wonder when money had changed hands.

So this is it, you realize. This is where that voice on the wind came from. Ne-el.

He is a large man in a three-piece suit and as his large hand closes the door behind you, you wonder what the arrangement was. Were they a home delivery service, like the ones that had just started up, delivering hot pizzas from Pizza Express, which is a job, you realize, you wouldn't have minded yourself, delivering pizzas instead of carrying a sandwich board advertising 2000 flats. But not, you realize, even in your wildest dreams, delivering young Irish youths to the furthest end of the Northern line. A pizza is one thing, you yourself are another. And you may not be this buyer's size, but you could make a fair mess of things if they got rough, and you can glimpse a kitchen at the end of the corridor, with probably a drawer and inside the drawer probably a breadknife. And as the front door clicks behind you, he opens another door, to his right, your left. You tell him you had been offered a place to sleep and needed to sleep, badly. You have a small backpack and would have happily kipped on the floor. But he leads you back into the plastic-wrapped living room, and pulls out the plastic-covered sofa, which turns into a bed. He comes in with a duvet then, or some blankets, spreads them over and leaves you there, closing the door behind him.

It seems horribly familiar. This strange plastic sofa, the same plastic over the matching chairs, like a houseproud next-door neighbour of yours, with a tiny, rabbit-eared television.

You turn off the light, get under the duvet. Try to fall asleep, but you can't get the financial transaction out of your mind. Did money change hands when you weren't looking, was it a matter of a bank draft for multiple deliveries, payment on the never-never, maybe the Levantine man gave the Scottish hippies Lebanese red and they repaid him with whomever they could befriend on the King's Cross platform, boys as well as girls, maybe it didn't matter. And maybe you had misunderstood the whole thing, maybe there was a flat in this repellent suburban home to be rented, with rooms for you, Peter Graham and his Clontarf girlfriend, whenever they made it to Euston Green. But the door opens, and you're disabused of all of these possibilities as the same gentleman enters in the darkness, now dressed in some kind of silk robe. As he lifts the duvet and falls, like an enormous walrus, beside you, you can only wonder again what kind of arrangement your two redeeming angels had come to with him. But the only question you can think to ask him is:

So you're a homosexual?

It seemed an appropriate enough word for the situation. The term gay hadn't entered the lexicon yet.

Good God no, he says. What made you think that?

The fact that you've crawled under the duvet beside me would be a hint.

And this is now getting comical.

Irish boys, he tells you, can make quite a bit of money round Piccadilly.

He has a south London accent, tinged with some sound of the Levant. A slight hint of a lisp.

I wasn't round Piccadilly, you tell him. They picked me up somewhere around King's Cross, and they asked me did I need a crash pad.

Still, he continues, Irish boys can make quite good money, if they clever about themselves.

You wonder what happened to the verb.

The conversation goes on for a bit, and you're nervous of sudden moves. This man's girth, his height, his muscular chest with its whorls of dark hair could subdue you if he wanted. But you let the silence form its own answer, and slip from under the duvet, whereupon he expressed surprise that you were still fully dressed.

You wonder where his surprise comes from. Maybe he expected something different. Maybe the misunderstanding was on your part, coming all this way, and now you're leaving, without any favours returned.

How was it meant to go, you wonder, some kind of sexual event, a price negotiated before or after, a return arrangement, with no further need to stroll the streets of Piccadilly. Maybe your paedophile could have explained it.

You wonder how much you were worth. Would it have paid for a down payment on a flat and helped the League for a Workers' Republic?

You make your way into the kitchen, which is like any disgusting suburban new-built kitchen and pull open the imitation wooden drawer and find a real knife there. Sharp blade, serrated edge. Would you have used it? Probably not. But as it was, you don't have to find out.

Your purchaser – would that be the word? Client, I suppose, if I had been willing – comes in and he is weeping. Tears, for his lack of tact, for this misunderstanding. He thought it had been all sorted out.

What had been sorted out?

He thought you knew the deal. An Irish boy picked up in Piccadilly should have known the deal.

King's Cross, you remind him. And you wonder does he have the name of the Scottish couple. No, he says, he pays them, they should have paid you, the way they pay all of the boys from Piccadilly.

No one paid me, you say, and it's time for me to go.

And he dries his tears. Turns out to be almost a gentleman. A great misunderstanding, he says.

Maybe, you tell him, you should ask for a refund. We have both been stiffed.

As with any misunderstanding, there is embarrassment in the air. So much embarrassment you could cut it with a knife. But not with this breadknife in the imitation wooden drawer. It was probably blunt anyway.

You can hear the dawn chorus outside. Pale suburban light is coming through the lace curtains over the windows.

Irish boys, he repeats, can make good money.

He still hasn't lost hope.

Round Piccadilly.

I'm sure they can, you tell him, but I have to leave now.

He seems about to cry again. And you really want to go.

What time is the first Tube?

He doesn't know.

Maybe I'll go there and wait.

So he opens the front door and bids you goodbye and you walk down the cramped suburban streets wondering how many boys that hippy couple have delivered to clients. Peace and love and good money to be made.

And thus began your hatred of hippies. Of suburban living rooms with pull-out sofas still wrapped in the factory plastic. Of the hippies who pretend love and friendship, who never share their dope or their crash pads and leave you back where you started, warming your hands on the fire with the hobos on Euston Green.

Breakfast on Pluto

I would put much of it in a film later. The central character wasn't me, but a trans naif from a Pat McCabe novel, played by Cillian Murphy. Kitten, the central character, didn't carry a sandwich board, but maybe she should have. Everything about the character was invented, but nothing about the context. I remembered so clearly the atmosphere, the grime, the sense of a manicured, ordered London life swirling around a transient one.

Because things were getting, as Kitten would say to Charlie in the same film, serious. Serious, serious, serious. I eventually found a squat, with a bunch of Northern Irish lads who watched their streets burn nightly on a stolen television. I overheard that Peter Green, who wrote 'Black Magic Woman', had had a bad trip in Munich. It was generally agreed that if Peter Green had left the building, things were getting serious. The other Peter, Graham, eventually did turn up with his student of German from Clontarf but the rambunctious squat in this building didn't suit them. They needed more discreet domestic arrangements. She got a secretarial job in the German Embassy. I later heard, and could hardly believe it, that the intention

Breakfast on Pluto. *Brendan Gleeson and*
Cillian Murphy, as wombles.

was to scope the German ambassador for a kidnapping. Peter
had moved beyond the polemical divisions between the LWR
and the IWG into rarer territory, only occupied by the Baader
Meinhofs and their Irish equivalents. He was found a year later,
tortured and bludgeoned to death by some aggrieved comrades
in a flat in St Stephen's Green, after an Easter Weekend.

Serious indeed.

Some years later again, I must have been married, because
I was coming out from a dentist's in Donnybrook who told
me 'your wife has an excellent mouth' when I heard the voice
again, coming from the nearby traffic.

Ne-el.

It sounded like a science fiction name. The ones given to characters with pointed ears and strange skin hues in bad space sagas. I looked around and thought I saw a bicycle turning the corner towards the new American Embassy. I felt a shiver, as if somebody in another galaxy had pressed a button and directed an electric shock into another version of me. What's wrong, Vivienne asked, and when I tried to explain, she only found it amusing. It's not that funny, I said. And she repeated the science fiction version of my name.

Ne-el.

But she couldn't get the separation of the two syllables right, or the thunderbolt of the surprise. She wasn't Zeus. She was too sweet for that. Maybe she was Juno.

Oedipus

By the time I'd returned, the college had moved, from Earlsfort Terrace to a building site across from RTÉ called Belfield. There was an ornamental pond without water in it, two towers of lecture halls and administrative buildings and a wasteland of diggers, cranes and yellow earthmoving behemoths that promised to build a campus. If they wanted to quash any communal sense of dissent, they couldn't have been more effective. But the basic question was, who had done this? I had moved from heaven to hell again. The basic order of things then was, if you were Catholic you went to UCD, if you were Protestant or English, you went to Trinity. But there had been something beautiful about that corner of St Stephen's Green, with the Georgian frontage of the old Newman Building, the byzantine-tiled church beside it and the unkempt gardens behind. Even more beautiful and out of time than the Trinity grounds down by College Green. You could access the Victorian pile on Earlsfort Terrace through this back door and know that James Joyce had done the same, told the dean of studies that an oil lamp was called a tundish in Lower Drumcondra, where they speak the best English. You could walk through the lost gardens with Vivienne, of the dark hair and the bluest of blue eyes, who grew up around Furry Park next to Roisin Sex, but whose family had moved, around the same time the college moved, to Southside Foxrock.

Whoever had done this was doing a number on the whole city. One of the only virtues of the policy of neutrality followed by De Valera was that the city had been spared the Blitz visited upon London. The only bombsite of your childhood was the waste ground around North Strand, where the bombers of the Luftwaffe had one night mistaken the lights of Dublin for Belfast, so the city you grew up in had the same fawn-coloured brick of the second city of the Empire, the same cobbled streets and pavements, the same Georgian piles, in Seán McDermott Street, Mountjoy Square and Henrietta Street gently sinking into their own demise, in their own time. But now what the Luftwaffe and the Führer hadn't done was being executed with far more efficiency by the architects of destruction of the Fianna Fáil Party. Did they hate the place, you had to wonder. Did they hate city life and everything that went with it? Or was there no avoiding this future of mechanical diggers, driven by lads in yellow jackets from Kiltimagh, leaving mounds of undigested mud in their wake?

You had to wander round it now, with your copy of *Ulysses* the only record of the city you grew up in. There was a boy you bonded with – we were all still boys, even in our late teens – going to the same lectures in those half-built corridors – Jim Sheridan, from Sheriff Street. He ran a theatre group, called SLOT Players. SLOT sounded urban and contemporary, but when you visited the premises they rehearsed in, you realized it stood for Saint Lawrence O'Toole, the patron of the hall in Sheriff Street. A bit like the way the Saint Francis Xavier became the SFX. Who were these saints, and why their ubiquity? Saint Vincent de Paul, Father Mathew, Blessed Oliver Plunkett, Saint Matt Talbot (no, he wasn't a saint yet), Saint Martin de Porres, better to initialize them, disguise them under the cloak of capital letters. Jim was from the house down the road from the Hall of Saint Lawrence O'Toole. You had always regarded theatre as the domain of well-spoken boys in tights, but there was an energy here that was infectious. And this skinny dynamo imbued even the idea of acting with the sulphurous danger of rock and roll. Together you executed a minor coup – took over the drama society in UCD and presented a version of *Oedipus Rex* in the old hall where the university used to be. Back in Newman House, what was called the Aula Maximus, next to the byzantine entrance of University Church. I call it a version, but it was more a deconstruction, a happening, an outrage done to the Sophocles text, over-influenced by the theories of the Living Theatre in New York and Jan Kott in Poland. We erected a scaffolding round the walls, leading to a raised stage on which a rock band was silhouetted. The audience had to submit to various indignities on the way in, prodded by nightsticks and flashlights through the total darkness into their seats, which were made of various tottering platforms hooked to the carapace of scaffolding so they could peer down at the floodlit wonders below. It was a safety hazard, probably a fire hazard, and always started late, as everything with Jim Sheridan did. I – you – played a version of Tiresias dressed in a gold lamé outfit that would have been more appropriate on Marc Bolan of T. Rex. The guts of this performance was a kind of ecstatic dance as the said Tiresias delivers, or is forced to deliver – I can't remember which now – the news that the murderer Oedipus is seeking is Oedipus himself. All accompanied by one of those endless guitar and drum solos that were popular at the time. Think of the Mothers of Invention by way of Emerson, Lake & Palmer with a overripe dollop of Deep Purple and you might get the idea. This formed the climax of Jim's version of the Sophocles original and the audience loved it. What we didn't know at the time was that the bulk of them had come from the five o'clock screenings of Stanley Kubrick's *2001: A Space Odyssey*, which was playing in the Grafton cinema down the road. It became a thing, apparently, to drop acid, attend the Kubrick space opera and, as the trip was wearing down, finish the evening with our version of *Oedipus Rex*. Which might account for the wide-eyed wonder that my trance/dance elicited. And for the fact that I never really acted again.

It was a rather wonderful diversion from the study of early Irish history and English literature in the building site down the dual carriageway.

We wrote a play together, based on the experiences of a lad we know from Seán McDermott Street who had spent his childhood in the orphanage of Artane. We gave it the uninspiring title of *Journal of a Hole*, a rather too obvious pun on the saintly journal of Pope John XXIII. It dealt with the whole gamut of themes of institutional abuse, physical, sexual and social. We presented it in the Project Arts Centre, which at the time (1971) was housed in an atmospheric basement in a building in Pearse Street. As usual with Jim, the director, the performance started late. We planted an actor – not me – dressed as a Christian Brother in the audience, who, when the play eventually ended, began spitting his objections to the performance from the back row. This led to retorts, declarations of support from the rest of the audience, and, of course, to headlines in the newspapers the next morning. So the play became a success, a kind of agitprop Brechtian piece of social commentary. And having dealt with the issue, in my kind of naivety, I thought others would deal with it too. I went to live in London, Los Angeles, returning intermittently to an Ireland that was changing, ever so slowly. So two decades later, when the horrors of abuse by church and state came into full public glare, when in fact it seemed to become the only theme of Irish fiction and dramaturgy, I was naive enough to think, didn't we write that all those years ago? There were screeds of abuse, there were some awkward headlines, but nobody arrested us. I was offered some of the scripts to direct. *The Magdalene Sisters*, *Philomena*, *The Secret Scripture*, *Song For a Raggy Boy*. But I had to wonder, why now? Is retrospective outrage more acceptable than contemporaneous outrage? Why weren't they written then?

America

We took the play to America. An Irish American philanthropist saw it in the Project in Pearse Street and invited us over. To Chicago, where he was meant to have booked some theatres, and then on to New York and some off-off-Broadway venue. We moved over there as a troupe and found ourselves beached in a mansion in a field in some suburb of Illinois.

So this was America, a continent that up to that date I had suspected never really existed. It was more a state of mind, an invention of the television, of various corporations who wanted to sell you things, of varieties of ice-cream and donut, the source of those dreadful baseball jackets that were sent over to certain friends of yours in Baymount Park, that had to be worn because they were cast-offs of cousins from America. We valued clothes from England, bum-freezer pea coats, tight jeans and winklepickers and Cuban heels. England, we knew, had some reality. Their football teams demanded our allegiance. But America was a dream I had seen on the movies, on the television in other people's houses, since we didn't, for a long time, own one ourselves. It was most typified for me by a series of white markings on a tarmac road, seen through a car window, heading west.

I remember the first thing I did there was kill a snake. I had never seen a snake before, and the snake seemed to belong to the same mythological realm as America itself. I walked out of the kitchen of the strange unfurnished mansion our philanthropist had put us in and the door swung backwards and forwards on its own hinges, the way doors never did at home. Into a field of some stubbled corn and I saw the serpent twisting its way around the roots. I grabbed a rock or a log and bashed its head in. I brought it back to the assembled troupe and said, look what I've found in this Garden of Eden, a snake. They were appalled, and then so was I. And maybe I had brought a hex down on us all.

The problem was, there were no theatres. It was Chicago, 1971, the memories of the riots were still raw. Our Irish American philanthropist brought us to the institutions he favoured. We played at Notre Dame University, in various halls and colleges he patronized, and realized how unregenerate the Irish American community could be. There would be no theatre in Chicago, no venue in New York, however far it might be from Broadway. We were introduced to Mayor Daly's cultural attaché, at one of those lunches that always seemed to be preceded by three martinis. What the hell was a martini, anyway? We were persuaded to perform at a Festival of Racial Harmony in the central square of Chicago, in front of the monumental sculpture that had been created from a cigarette paper cutout by Picasso. There was a gospel choir, there were various brass bands and there was me, for some reason, as I was always relied on for musical solutions, playing a jig on the banjo-mandolin into the enormous speakers while the theatre group did some business behind me which ended in the Black Power salute. We were thrown off the stage, of course, and our Chicago sojourn came to an appropriate conclusion. But not before we met some activists from the Southside, who wore the obligatory camouflage military fatigues and the black berets. They had admired our performance, in particular the banjo and the clenched salute. We were desperate for a venue, a theatre, an audience. Could we maybe perform in some venues of theirs, and, by the way, did they have guns to go with those outfits? No was the answer to the first, and yes to the second.

So we went home. But I can still remember the dotted white line on the highway that seemed to head west, all the way to Los Angeles, California. I was sorely tempted to follow it and I couldn't work out why. I knew nothing of Hollywood and can only wonder what would have happened if I had gone there. Nineteen seventy-one, West Hollywood. *Easy Rider* had been and gone. *The Godfather* had just opened. I saw it in Chicago with Jim and he said they'll be quoting that line forever. That one about the offer he can't refuse.

But Irish people didn't make movies. Italians did, cigar-smoking Americans did. The French did, in their impossibly beautiful apartments, drinking coffee from their handleless cups. What we did was we wrote, because a pen and paper cost nothing. We scribbled down plays, scrabbled together costumes out of old castoffs and, if we were lucky enough, found a venue to perform in.

Lit.

So back to the building site and the wind whipping round the ornamental lake and those strange canvas carpeted halls that led to massive lecture theatres and a buttery across the way where boys from the country ate enormous plates of chips, sometimes garnished with melted chocolate. Maybe because they couldn't do the same at home. And maybe it's better to think of yourself as a fictional character, given how strange it all seems. Huge cantilevered rows of seats leading to a semi-circular stage where the enormously tall but decidedly elegant Denis Donoghue talks about John Donne's 'space-age mentality'. His pirouettes and hand gestures are oddly feminine in so etiolated a figure. Seamus Deane, smaller but equally elegant and with a movie star's good looks, talks about tropes in Dickens. What on earth is a trope? You listen to him tear an innocent apart for admitting to enjoyment of Dylan Thomas. Apparently Dylan Thomas doesn't have the rigorous intellectual spine that is the hallmark of great literature. But he enjoyed it, you think to yourself, and what's the point of literature if not enjoyment? These I. A. Richards enthusiasts don't even have to like what they read, they just have to analyse it.

And analysis demands a certain kind of complexity. You begin to enjoy Proust, who is defiantly complex and meet a lecturer in drama in the college bar, who is boning up on Proust for his next tutorial. Wonderful, you say, and ask him about the expanse of yellow in the painting Charles Swann was viewing when the Duchesse de Guermantes invited him to her next season's salon. What painting could that have been? Oh, I haven't time to read Proust, the lecturer tells you. I'm so busy with the secondary literature.

Aha. Analysis and enjoyment seem anathema, one to the other. So you turn your attention to history. Medieval and early Irish, which won't destroy any prior enjoyment you might have taken, since you know so little about either of them. You're introduced to a world of illustrated manuscripts, courtly romance and genealogical detective work. To a fascinating character who sits in an office with a Siamese cat on his lap, behind a wall full of Chinese illustrated scrolls. The professor of early Irish history, Francis John Byrne. He reads Latin, Greek, Persian, Mandarin and Cantonese, German, French, Icelandic and, of course, what scraps of early and medieval Irish can be gleaned from the texts. A small, delicate figure with an enormous head, he lives with his mother in one of those strange flats off the dual carriageway near Belfield. He has written a book, *Irish Kings and High-Kings*, with the best first sentence of any that you have come across. It begins, like all great first sentences, in media res, throws you right into the action and creates an itch, an anxiety, even, to know more. It is up there with Kafka's 'As Gregor Samsa awoke one morning from uneasy dreams he found himself transformed into an enormous insect.' With Carson McCuller's, 'In the town there were two mutes, and they were always together.' Even with Dickens's 'It was the best of times, it was the worst of times.'

'There was an increasing tendency in the eleventh century for the term "Ui Neill" to be confined to the kings of the North, a usage reinforced by their descent from Niall Caille (846) and by the posthumous prestige of Niall Glundub (919), grandfather of the O'Neill: Domnall's son Aed Ua Neill (1004) and the latter's nephew Flaithbertach were the first to make a surname of Domnall's papponymic.'

OK. What does papponymic even mean? Something to do with being named after your grandfather. It seems odd to abandon literature for the minutiae of early Irish genealogies, but you are already hooked. Like a medieval forensic detective picking his way through what remains of a vanished world, you become fascinated and then obsessed. You have to read comparative studies, of societies at similar stages of development and are soon knee-deep into Lévi-Strauss, structural anthropology and hagiographical texts from the seventh and eighth centuries. You write a thesis on these, the strange amalgam of paganism, magic and piety in these quasi-biblical tales. They will form the subterranean background to a novel, many, many years later, *The Well of Saint Nobody.*

Marriage

We had a bungalow, a beautiful bungalow, on Victoria Road, on an odd little triangle between the Howth and the Malahide roads. Half Clontarf and half Fairview. The bungalows were kinds of cousins to the bungalows in Killester, built for demobbed soldiers after the First World War, called, for some impenetrable reason, the Middle Third. Maybe ours was in the Beginning Third or the End Third? It was once serviced by the Contemptible Bus Company, whose name was at least traceable, as it serviced the homes of the Old Contemptibles, a reference to the Kaiser's dismissal of 'Sir John French's contemptible little army', the BEF, or the British Expeditionary Force.

Vivienne was my wife's name and I did her the great disservice of marrying her, but only after numerous attempts to avoid that fate. Come to England was the first one, come to Spain the next, that little island called Formentera from which I'd written you those first love letters before returning to that grim building site that was UCD. Did I ever get replies? I can't remember, maybe her ardour was less than mine, or didn't need words, which would have been odd since all we read was poetry. She came from the other end of Clontarf, around Furry Park, and had the bluest of eyes and a face I could and did swim in. But why marriage? Because of this massive, burning need to be together. Because everyone was doing it, Shay to Fran and Vinnie to Felicia and Shay's brother Peter to Sheila. You're too young to do this, my father said until he met her and kind of fell in love in turn. Her father, who was wealthier than mine, bought her – and us – that bungalow after returning from the London we should have escaped to in the first place.

We had returned for a funeral. The Dublin and Monaghan bombings had claimed her aunt in Talbot Street. Her father had to identify the dreadful remains and I don't think her uncle Leo ever recovered. We took the boat back from Holyhead and every passenger on the crowded deck was returning to bury a dismembered body. Twenty-six people died in the Dublin bombings and it would have been hard to count the extended members of those inner city families, but it did seem that they all had emigrated to England and every one of them was on that boat. It was like a rain-lashed ship of furies. The women – and it was mostly women I talked to – cursed the country that had forced them into exile and dragged them back to mourn dead relatives. A funeral then, in Cavan, where her people were from and, once back, we stayed.

So, the house. I wonder would a demobbed member of the Old Contemptibles have had a better time than I did in that house. I can't imagine he would. I was a house husband with a beautiful wife who was always in search of a career. She worked as a teacher at first, then as a lawyer, apprenticed to her father's firm, and I had the rare pleasure of meeting her in the Four Courts, in a three-piece striped corporate suit surrounded by bewigged barristers, who seemed to find her as desirable as I did. I had no perceptible career other than a desire to write. So I did that, between odd jobs, scribbling on the kitchen table, looking after one child, the golden-haired Sarah, and then another, the dark-haired Anna. What strange, unstructured and innocent bliss it was. It couldn't and didn't continue, of course: the stresses were too acute, on her, in particular, as a working mother. Bob's shop across the road, a street the kids could play on before and after school. The entire seafront across the North Wall exploded one night. Nothing to do with the UVF or the IRA: the oil terminals on the docks across the bay had caught fire. We walked down to the seafront, gaberdine coats over pyjamas, and watched the docklands aflame, as if the end of the world had come. It was a strangely happy apocalypse, though, the whole seafront crowded with awakened dreamers watching the fire and that odd sense of an eruptive event bringing total strangers together. I wondered would the end of the world be as comforting as this.

The world almost ended then, several days later. I was scribbling at the old pine table, had brought Sarah to school, and Anna, too young as yet for school, was playing on the street. I heard the sound every parent dreads. A screech of brakes, a scream, a dull thump.

I ran out of the kitchen door and saw a girl lying on the roadway, a small blue corduroy dress, tiny brown shoes and a pool of blood around her inert head. There was an ashen-faced policeman in a state of shock, his motorbike lying on the pavement. I lifted her up, although I probably shouldn't have, and for some reason tried to reassure him, as he told me how she ran out straight in front of him. We had her in an ambulance within minutes, and her screams of protests when the doctor tried to examine her convinced him that she would be OK, could be taken home safely. Who felt the most guilt, Vivienne because she wasn't there or me because I was? It was a hard one to work out. A bit like marriage, I supposed. There were continual knocks at the kitchen door, of neighbours offering their condolences. She's fine, we assured them. At least we hope she is. Until a dark-haired man from across the road, who had always kept a rather sinister, watchful eye on the kids playing in the street, insisted on reading my cards. That was the kind of time it was, the seventies, you threw the sticks for the *I Ching*, had your horoscope elaborately tracked, became expert in tarot and table-tapping. This gentleman, anyway, fanned out a conventional pack of cards and as a strategy, I supposed, of reassurance to a parent who had almost suffered a bereavement, asked me to pick one. He was a proficient and wise reader, he told me, and I had no option but to take one. He took one look at it, returned it to the pack and said, I'm sorry, I have to go. Aren't you going to give me that reading? I asked him. How many cards did you take? He asked me. One, like you said.

No, he said. You took three.

And the door slammed and I was left there on the red tufty carpet. What did that mean, three cards? To what awful destiny was I condemned? Would Anna ever recover? Would Vivienne ever forgive herself? Would I?

I'd see him on the street in the coming weeks and months, and always avoid him, as my daughter grew back to full, ungovernable health. She was beautiful and delightful, but obsessed by imaginary friends. They populated the kitchen like a ring of invisible fairies. I'd enter the front door and she'd say – hey, you're stepping on Jessica's frock.

Sorry, I'd say and gingerly tread my way into the kitchen proper and she'd say, now you're on Lucy's shoe. And Lucy's mother just bought her those shoes.

On my way across the floor, making a delicate dance around these non-existent creatures, I'd wonder, would things have been different if I had only taken one card? The ace of spades, the queen of hearts, it didn't matter, but would the mistake of taking three be that indefinable thing, that objective correlative, to use the phrase I had learned in those drab English lectures, of our future life together? Like the witches in *Macbeth*? By the pricking of my thumb...

Something wicked did come. The house was sold, she moved to Ranelagh, I moved to Bray and got to walk along the same promenade my mother walked along with my two daughters. But was it anything to do with those three cards?

In a piece of fiction it would have been. I had already begun to write them. Stories, the first one of which still chills me with its bleakness. Called 'Last Rites', it deals with an Irish labourer in London who works on a demolition site (as I did), lives in a one-room squat without a shower (as we did) and has to wash the grime from his body in the public shower in a bathhouse in Kensal Rise (as many did) and cuts his wrists there, as he listens to the echoing conversations around him.

Labour

I was in the labour exchange in Gardener Street, inching forward with a line of men towards the man with the brown envelope who would give you your brown envelope with your dole for the next week. All men. Was there a women's labour exchange? Maybe, but I can't imagine it. It was the seventies after all. I was carrying a brown paper bag myself, as were most of the men around me. They could have had anything in their brown paper bags: copies of the Bible, of *Das Kapital*, of Mickey Spillane, a pair of welder's gloves or a spanner but the presumption was that the brown paper bag contained sandwiches. Anything else would imply you were not available for employment, which is what, of course, being unemployed is all about.

I definitely had books in my paper bag and one of those school copybooks I used to scribble things in with the small map of Ireland on the back. I had employment, too, of a kind, as I'm sure had most of the men in the line with me. I was a floating member of a theatre group and my duties there consisted of scribbling occasional scenes in my copybook and accompanying the resultant scenes with music, mainly on the saxophone, which I was learning to play at the time. Others in this itinerant group were Jim Sheridan, who would become better known as a film director; his brother Peter; Vinnie McCabe; Garrett Kehoe, an actor; and Paula Meehan and Desmond Hogan, both later to become distinguished writers. (A writer is nothing if not distinguished.) I had a serviceable degree in English and History, but no possibility of employment. Again, it was the seventies. I had applied to the National Film School in Britain, submitting some of what I'd written, and to my amazement had been given a place. The costs were so prohibitive that I couldn't afford to go, and there was no scholarship aid. Unlike my friend Mucky Dunne, now battling vodou houngans in a village in Haiti, I couldn't access English grants.

We were most of us married. Children, really, soon to be with children, helplessly in love and helplessly unemployed. But why marriage? It was almost incomprehensible. In the seventies it was what you did. What was the alternative? Go to London, Paris, Berlin or Rome and live like Modigliani in a garret? How would you even get there? But even that doesn't explain it. In the end I think it might have been some strange imitative urge. Others are doing it so why shouldn't you?

But at least, having been married, you had a suit. One of those wide-lapelled jobs, with flared trousers that would look incomprehensible today, as odd as a high-waisted Victorian number with a wing collar. You wore it to the wedding with your beloved child bride, Vivienne. She wore an otherworldly assembly of crushed green velvet, which made her blue eyes even more startling. Green was an unlucky colour, somebody told you, but you replied that you didn't believe in superstitions. But if you didn't believe in superstitions, what on earth were you doing in this unlovely hall, this absolute shrine to superstitions, with the new-made mosaics of the stations of the cross adorning the walls. You used to like religion. You used to even, if you remember your childhood years, believe in it. You remember those nuns with their bowing head-dresses and the late spring sunlight shimmering through the sycamore tree and the certainty that God was in His heaven and all was right with the world. In fact, you believed so strongly then that you found this ritualistic, absurd and quite unmagical ceremony offensive. What were these motions, what were those blessings, what was that aged cleric in his gold embossed apron doing when lifting something from the chalice and the entire audience shuffling to their knees – I know audience is the wrong word, congregation, but they behaved like a bad audience at a mediocre play that maybe once had some meaning – if they didn't believe in it? There would be a punishment, you felt, some ferociously biblical one for such lack of engagement.

I wore that same suit at an interview for the only job that seemed to be available, as a supply teacher in a German school on the Southside. The principal, Herr something or other, by the strangest of coincidences, happened to be wearing the same suit. Exactly the same suit, probably bought in the same shop in Henry Street. He wore it better, being broad shouldered and from Berlin and, to his great regret, took it as a sign.

I was a bad teacher. Maybe in another school I might have functioned better, but in this Germanic school, I was a dreadful teacher. I wore the suit as often as I could, but that fooled nobody, least of all the pupils, and while, individually, they could be adorable (they were barely out of pre-school) like any group in a pack who sense a weakness, they proved merciless. I was torn to pieces by a group of bilingual nine year olds. And fired.

Eventually, I took the only other job that was available. As a railway porter in the CIÉ railway yard in East Wall, bordering the river and the docks. I would cycle past Gouldings fertilizer factory, where the odour of coal tar would burn your nostrils. Women, clustering with children round the imposing metal gates. Waiting for their husbands, you thought, though it seemed a bit early. Maybe for the husbands coming off the night shift? But no, you were told when you finally reached the railway yard, called the Point Depot. They were mothers of children with asthmatic problems, for whom the inhalation of coal tar provided some rumoured relief. Hopefully not accompanied by a spot on the lung.

I was employed for some reason in the railway yard, but there was nothing whatsoever to do. Wander round those empty carriages with a brush, the supervisor told you. Fall asleep, if you find an empty sack or two. Read a book? No, for Jaysus' sake, put that book in a brown paper bag, pretend it's your lunch.

The only excitement happened on those random days when the carriages were full, with random produce unloaded from the cargo ships docked on the Liffey, nearby. A bounty of hair dryers, one day. Of electrical coil, the next. All of this contraband shifted down the line, across the tracks, underneath the blue serge railway porter's uniform, tossed over the wall onto Sheriff Street Upper.

It was an innocuous form of idleness, probably designed to keep the numbers in the Gardiner Street dole line down, and it soon came to an end. CIÉ was rationalizing.

So maybe this was the punishment. For the three cards, for the agnostic wedding, for everything.

I would shuffle forwards in that dole queue with my books and my scribbled copybook, and reach the end of the line. The supervising officer looks at me, from behind the glass booth. He checks my dole card against his list of names. But he is looking a little too long, and I'm getting nervous. He says, give me a minute, and vanishes into one of the doors behind painted, the way everything is painted in the Gardiner Street dole offices, in various shades of official green.

The line behind me shifts. There are subdued coughs and the flares of several matches, as cigarettes are lit and butts relit. They have already been waiting long enough.

The supervising officer re-emerges from the green door – although it's more of a brown, stained by generations of supervising officers' handprints and a dulled, tobaccoey hue. He has a small file in his hand, in, surprisingly, a dull green folder. He opens it, and takes out a newspaper clipping. It is a picture of me, in a fish-suit, playing the saxophone. It is there to illustrate an article on street theatre, a new phenomenon in Dublin at the time. And it was the seventies, after all. The fish-suit is really a pair of dyed long johns with scales painted on them. And some kind of papier-mâché jaws over my head. All that is visible of me is my lips, teeth clamped over the saxophone mouthpiece. How he recognizes me, me, I have no idea. But there I was, apparently gainfully employed with a bunch of actors on a Dublin street, and here I am now, collecting unemployment benefit.

I look at his face behind the glass booth, the dusty governmental green walls behind him. He asks is this you.

I could lie. I could come up with a smart ass answer. You could say, prove it. But I admit, it is me. Or it was me, last Wednesday.

He places the brown envelope with the dole money and the page of newsprint into the file and says he will have to consider taking legal action. I think, great, I'm about to be arrested for playing the saxophone dressed in a fish-suit. But I feel a sudden, irrational surge of exhilaration. It must be what bank robbers feel when they've finally copped it. What adulterers feel when their love nest has been busted. You're neither a bank robber nor an adulterer, but you like this new feeling and you want it to continue.

Do you really have to do that? I ask him.

I'll be obliged to, he says, if you take this envelope.

Fuck the envelope, you think and the money inside it.

But what you actually say is, you won't.

You mean you won't collect unemployment benefit while being gainfully employed?

I will neither collect unemployment benefit, nor be gainfully employed, you tell him.

You mean that? he asks.

I do, you tell him.

But what you really mean is, you are done stuffing your copies of Jean Genet in a brown paper bag, pretending they are margarine sandwiches, shuffling forwards in this most depressing of halls to see your supervising officer's face behind the glass. There has to be something better than this.

And you walk back, through that once majestic structure, past the lines of men with their brown paper bags. The Georgian windows are tall and elegant and the sun is streaming through them, catching the shuffling dust and the cigarette smoke although the walls are still that horrible governmental green, and you wonder is there a word for this new feeling. If there isn't, you'll have to write it.

Trans

The theatre group was called the Children's T Company, an offshoot of the theatrical dabblings of Jim Sheridan, his brother Peter, me and a group of Dublin actors. It achieved two things. Some semblance of an undeclared living for most of us, along with the dole. And a haphazard sense of social engagement. We were bringing theatre to 'the people'. 'The people' meant a crowd of random tourists and puzzled pedestrians at the top of Grafton Street. Or a series of playgrounds in the flats of the inner city, where the kids would generally tear our costumes and our papier-mâché props to pieces, and this kind of mayhem blended with our theatrical style to create something like a 'happening'. We became experts in a kind of manufactured mayhem. Or in the pretence that the chaos our presence brought to these communities had some broader social purpose. I was put in charge of the musical accompaniments to these shows, hence the fish-suit, the papier-mâché fish mask and the saxophone. I built a vast, mobile assembly of percussion instruments on a wheeled wooden base, old metal barrels, tangled sheets of corrugated iron, whatever bass drums and snares we could get our hands on, theatrical thunder sheets and a huge array of implements with which to beat this percussive sculpture. Kids could whack and boom and shiver and rattle, and create some kind of score to the circus in front of them. It was exhausting, seemed to drive our audiences into something approaching riot, and left us sweating and filthy, but was great fun. Until we did a day-long production on Dollymount Strand.

I had the idea of presenting an open-ended version of the W. B. Yeats play *The Cat and the Moon* among the dunes beyond the Bull Wall. Of taking the basic story, and stretching into an afternoon-long performance, involving the core of the kids who had become our audience. A blind man and a lame man wander the backroads of Sligo, in search of a saint who can effect a cure. Simply that, played by our actors, with an assortment of costumes and props that would allow the kids to find their way into the drama. The blind man, played by Fergus Cronin, spent the afternoon exploring the issue of what sight was with the kids.

Where are we?

The dunes, Dollymount Strand.

What are dunes?

Kind of little mountains of sand, beside the sea.

And by the way, what is the sea?

It's there in front of you, you mad blind thing, that blue yoke over the way.

Blue? What's blue?

It's a colour, like red.

Explain to me what a colour is?

The kids dressed in different costumes, to add to the confusion, or the illusion. One of them was a natural actor, a thin boy from the Sheriff Street flats, who made a great comic display of wearing the girls' dresses. And amazingly, the performances and the whole event – to call it a play would be really stretching the form – kept us going until sundown. Until the moment came when our afflicted actors – one blind, one lame – met the saint.

The saint was played by Garret Kehoe, and in a nod to Samuel Beckett, was dwelling in a metal rubbish bin hidden deep among the dunes.

The lame man is the first to notice him – he can see, remember? – and is cured, to do his version of a break dance in the sand. Up across the dunes and away.

The blind man comes next. A healing hand across his eyelids and abracadabra, he can see. But so convincing had been the suspension of belief, or maybe Fergus's acting, that the kids were almost moved to tears at being recognized by their previously blind beggar.

And the event is over, it's getting dark, a van trundles up to take the audience away. We're wrapping up the props, when we wonder why Garret is still stuck in his rubbish bin, and we hear a voice, and it's praying.

The boy from the flats, his skinny frame still clad in a girl's costume dress, is kneeling by the rubbish bin. Making a heart-rending plea to Garret, who is frozen stiff by his words.

Please saint, he says, make me a girl. I know I'll go back home and I'll wake in the morning and my da will beat me again, tell me he wanted a boy for a son, not a daughter, or whatever I've turned out to be. I saw you make the blind man see, and all I'm asking is that when I go home and after we have our tea and he whacks me to bed, make it that I'll wake up as a girl. Then he'd know what I am, and he'll have no more reason to beat me and everyone would know what I am and the whole thing will stop. I know you can do this, saint, because I saw you make the blind man see and the cripple walk. I'm going to go to bed, go to sleep and when I open my eyes, I'll be a girl and it'll all be allright for ever and ever.

The tears were streaming down Garret's face, as he does his best to explain that he's not a saint, just Garret Kehoe, an actor. And what's wrong with being a feminine boy? No, I'm not a boy, the kid continues, I'm a girl inside, I just seem to be a boy, and I know you can make it happen, saint. Maybe I should talk to your father. No, you can't do that, he'd bate the face of you, the way he does with me. And you don't have to do it now, this minute. Just tell me that when I wake up tomorrow, I'll wake up as a girl...

Was it the power of illusion, of storytelling, or the extremity of the dilemma? He/she believed they could be 'cured'. Could at least be saved another beating. A cure that nowadays would be called a transition. Here was a natural comic, who had kept them entertained with a version of a drag act the whole afternoon. But there was no Tavistock Clinic then, and the term 'gender dysphoria' probably hadn't been thought of. What was heartbreakingly clear was that the Children's T Company couldn't work that miracle.

Backlot

I had published a book of short stories and written one script for a movie that was made, called *Traveller*. The short stories caused a stir, they were reviewed extensively and I will never forget sitting on the RTÉ book programme with the august Seán Ó Faoláin, waiting for his judgement. Why they paired the first-time writer with the most revered on national television was a bit of a puzzle. Maybe the spectacle of my public humiliation would make interesting viewing. Mr Ó Faoláin was dressed in tweed, as most writers were then. I don't remember what I was wearing. But what I do remember was the curt politeness with which he greeted me before the cameras started rolling, so I sat there, waiting for my evisceration. Then an outpouring of praise began that had my jaw dropping. I began to sweat. When he pronounced his judgement on the title story, as 'one of the best since, or indeed before Joyce', I did begin to wonder what planet he was on and how I would survive this accolade.

I began a novel soon afterwards, which would now probably read like a parallel to the early pages of this memoir. It was called *The Past*, about an attempt to construct a narrator's past through photographs. Frozen images, memory, holiday towns in Bournemouth and Bray, as if the butterfly wings of pivotal events could echo through long-dead characters. This one dealt with the aftermath of the War of Independence. I would write another about its aftermath in turn, Ireland during the Second World War 'Emergency', called *Sunrise with Sea Monster*. I would write yet another about the period preceding all of these, called *Shade*. I would write fiction about everything but the present

But I could write about the present in film scripts.

I can still remember standing with Jim Sheridan by the railings on St Stephen's Green and seeing a traveller wedding tumble out of University Church. The groom looked too young to be out of short pants and the bride even younger. They headed towards the back of a Hiace van, held open by a burly father in an ill-fitting dress suit. It must have struck us both, since a story popped into my mind, as it must have popped into his. He would many years later write and produce a script called *Into the West*.

I began sketching out a story, on the kitchen table in Victoria Road. An arranged marriage between two kids, too young to know anything about life, let alone sex. The father of the bride runs a trade in the scavengings from burned-out shops and houses in Belfast from the market in Jonesboro, just over the border. He needs this marriage because the prospective groom is an expert mechanic and can keep his fleet of vans on the road. After the child wedding, they drive on their honeymoon to Jonesboro, to pick up a batch of transistor radios and another delivery of televisions from Belfast. They can barely stand each other's company, but a series of mishaps gradually draws them together. The boy comes across a gun on his travels, and in an encounter with his father-in-law, whom they both have come to resent, even hate (I seem to remember a horse whip), he shoots him dead. Thereby, with a big dollop of influence from J. M. Synge, gaining his new wife's admiration for the first time. They find out about sex on a rubbish tip, overlooking the margarine factory across the Boyne river in Drogheda. And move on to other adventures

What immediately became clear to me, sketching out this little scenario, was that nothing in it would have ever crept into the prose I was writing. There was melodrama, action, absurdity, and an absolute freedom from the rather crippling influence of the 'Irish Literary Tradition'. And images, so many of them. I remembered that white line in Chicago, heading all the way to California. I remembered me and Jim dreaming of movies, which seemed to be only made by extravagant Italians, intellectual Frenchmen or Americans with big cigars. The plays we would produce, and the rather sniffy comments, that they were 'too filmic'.

And I began to understand that old attraction.

I finished the script, it was read by an Irish film-maker called Joe Comerford who had made some short films that I admired. It was also read by BBC Birmingham, who produced a series called *Play For Today*. The BBC wanted to buy it. Joe Comerford wanted to buy it, but, unlike the BBC, had no money to do so. I introduced Joe to the BBC, who were happy to have him as a director. But he wasn't happy. Saw this as a film, not a sixty-minute TV play. Persuaded me to give it to him, and foolishly I said yes.

I won't go into the subsequent debacle, which would be repeated many years later, with the Donald Trump of Irish dramatic production, other than to say that it showed me that a writer with any interest in film should avoid it altogether or get their hands on a camera.

The finished film bore no relationship to the script I had written. It was almost entirely devoid of horse-whippings, gunplay and sex in a rubbish tip overlooking the Boyne river. *Gun Crazy*, it definitely was not. Neither, oddly enough, despite its grim hand-held realism, did it have any hint of the turbulent island we were living in at the time.

So I was surprised to get a call from Ardmore Studios. I took a train to Bray and walked from the seafront station up the hill from the town to the swing barrier thing that admitted the cars. I walked past it, past a few buildings that looked like warehouses, through a bunch of Portakabins to what seemed to be the front office. I assumed it was the front office because there was a mud-spattered Rolls-Royce parked in front of it, as casually as if it had been a Morris Minor. I walked in and met John Boorman. He had read my stories, and had read the script, but probably hadn't seen the finished film.

We began a conversation that continues, intermittently, to this day. He brought me to lunch (lunch!) in the studio commissary. (It had one then.) He gave me a book to read, which he was thinking of turning into a movie. We began swapping ideas, as an assortment of individuals drifted through his office, the commissary and his life. I suppose now you would call them the 'glitterati'. Peter Ustinov, one day. Christopher Isherwood and his boyfriend (!) Don Bachardy the next.

The book was an odd one, written about an imaginary Ireland by a Frenchman, called *Le Voyage de John O'Flaherty*. Writing this now draws me back into a strange world of half-realized fantasies, odd dreams that shouldn't be compelling but absolutely are, and the thrill of taking a real world apart and replacing it with an imagined one. It was about a magician who learns to make things disappear. That was the one idea which remained in our journey through it. John, who was the absolute master of generic, realistic cinema, as anyone who has seen *Point Blank* and *Deliverance* should know, had this strange urge to go in the opposite direction of his strengths. Into metaphor. And maybe we are all like that. We are told what we are good at, and want to do the opposite. His greatest movies have turned the absolutely real world, by force of his camera's engagement with it, into metaphoric force fields. His worst are the ones that are unmoored by any realistic land-scape. I watched them all, working on this script with him and we came up with this wonderfully odd fable, rooted in what would now be drearily called a post-apocalyptic world, but it was a real world. Shards of a Dublin that might one day exist. The alleyways around the Olympia Theatre became part of the drama, the theatre itself became the music hall environment where the magic happened. And what was the magic? A magi-cian, from a family of magicians, used to creating illusions of objects vanishing and disappearing, learns to make things actually vanish. And for some reason (the logic of which I can't actually remember) this vanishing act leaves a ripple of desire behind it. In a world where the detritus of 'things' – discarded things – seems to have created its own wasteland, the act of liberating the world of 'things' becomes its own liberation.

A conjurer's clock is the first object to fly into oblivion. Afterwards, a host of beloved, talismanic objects. Then a bird. Then an individual. Then the magician's own father. Where have they gone? There is no answer, no resolution. A screen, cluttered with objects, landscapes, animals, people, gradually clears itself, washes itself back into white

Insane, perhaps. But I had fun doing it. And I blame myself for his subsequent obsession. John would spend years trying to mount this project, make a string of films in between times, but always return to it. River Phoenix was attached, John Hurt, Ben Kingsley, Caleb Landry Jones.

But after we had finished that script, and probably after his first attempt to mount it, he presented me with another. *Excalibur*, written by him and a gent called Rospo Pallenberg (even the name sounded exotic). Based on *Le Morte d'Arthur* of Sir Thomas Malory. And this was big. Insanely big, 400 pages, I think, the draft he handed me. He asked me to go through the script with him, as a kind of editor-cum-uncredited writer. I was thrilled to do that, paid some money and began the daily trek for the railway station in Bray up the long road to the studios. The string of Portakabins round the back which constituted the offices. So I gradually began to share his obsession with the Grail legends, his determination to tell the whole of the Malory story, from the days of Uther Pendragon and the magician Merlin's discovery of the sword Excalibur through to the arrival of Arthur, his release of the sword from the stone, the establishment of Camelot and the Knights of the Round Table, the disintegration of that unity and the search for the Grail.

I'm exhausted even listing these elements, which read like the kind of project that would these days make a Netflix series, and in fact has more than once been made, to generally dreadful effect. But John's muscular determination was infectious; it was a project that seemed to have lived with him for years. He had attempted to make *The Lord of the Rings*, and failed. Elements of the archetypes in the legend had informed his more popular movies. He described to me how even *Point Blank* has a Merlin figure, manipulating the elements of the plot from behind the scenes. I rewatched the end of *Deliverance*, saw the hand emerging from the lake dreamed by John Voight at the end. The problem was that these mythical dreamlike eruptions happened in stories of wrenching realism, which somehow added to their force. Within these 400 pages there was nothing but myth. And the elements could grow, and did grow, through European legend and literature, like a kind of self-generating virus. Tristran and Isolde, the entirety of Romance courtly literature, Wolfram von Eschenbach's *Parzival*, *Gawain and the Green Knight*, even Wagner's Ring Cycle. John's script touched on them all, and we went through it like two pathologists, trying to strip back the excess flesh and find the connective skeletal tissue underneath. And in the process of doing this I rewatched *Star Wars* and saw George Lucas's version of the same, set in a galaxy far far away. It had an undiscovered Arthur, of course, Luke Skywalker, with a destiny hidden from him (like Wolfram von Eschenbach's Parzival), it had a Merlin figure who knew that secret destiny called Obi-Wan Kenobi, it even had a light sabre doing duty as Excalibur. And I thought if George Lucas can reduce centuries of legendary half-myths into ninety minutes of entertainment, why can't we? I came back with a plan, concocted on the train from Raheny to Bray to reduce those 400 pages into something more manageable, more elemental, and John said, well that's it, I'm off to make the movie.

You can't, I thought.

But of course he could. He wanted me around, though, even if the script work wasn't finished. Maybe *because* the script work wasn't finished. To bounce ideas off me, as he wrestled with this gargantuan story that seemed determined to spread and metastasize. I came up with a plan, to make a documentary about this very thing. It would be fascinating to observe, and maybe to document. John wrestling with this unruly, unfinished creature. The making of *Excalibur*.

It was an extraordinary act of generosity, in retrospect. He shaved off a portion of his budget so I could hire a camera crew. Allowed me access to every facet of the production. I couldn't afford the National Film School, after I'd left college. And now he provided me with one.

I had no idea about the business of films, apart from the experience of being carried away by them, in the Astor, the Academy, the Fairview, or the Scouts hall in Dollymount, where I saw *Abbott and Costello Meet Frankenstein*, projected onto a badly stretched sheet over our heads as we sat ·on benches. But I can still remember the sight of a furred hand creeping through a kitchen or a bathroom door and the terror it induced. Wasn't it meant to be a comedy? The sound of Bela Lugosi (or was it Christopher Lee?) flying as a bat towards Mina's window terrified me even more. A kind of electric hum, as I remember, that seemed to be echoed by the sound that came from the concrete-encased generators in Fairview Park as we walked home from the Fairview Cinema. That sound terrified me for two solid years, seemed to be everywhere, from the whistling of the wind heard through the trees outside my bedroom, to the electricity pylons that ran past the Bull Wall. In fact what could be heard induced far more terror than what could be seen. What you saw was fixed and enclosed somehow, what you heard could fill your imagination, be echoed by the random sounds of the average suburb. The first movie I ever saw I traced, not by any image, but by a sound. It was called *Them*, and I was brought to it for some reason by my mother. About giant, nuclear-irradiated ants taking over Los Angeles. I can remember the image of a landscape of sand dunes, remarkably similar to the sand dunes of Dollymount Strand. Then, a strange, piercing electronic moan – though moan hardly describes it, more like a high-pitched, otherworldly screech with a recurrent, almost mechanical beat – and over the dunes would stalk giant ants. The ants were hardly impressive, obviously enlarged Oxford Scientific versions of the real thing. But the sound made them terrifying.

Here, on the backlot of Ardmore Studios, which would soon be transformed into a suburb of Bray, was the business of film. Actors on horseback, dressed in gleaming armour, charging through a burning forest landscape towards a camera on tracks. I knew most of them. Liam Neeson, Gabriel Byrne, Niall O'Brien, Brid Brennan, Mannix Flynn. Cutting short their charge – one of them had fallen, the fire had gone out, the camera had jammed. Doing it again, and again, and again. It's strange to recount, when everyone has an iPhone and can track their camera over a dish on a dinner table, how cumbersome, how laborious but how absolutely magical it seemed. That Panaflex camera, hoisted onto a dolly by muscular dudes in shorts, the lenses themselves, enormous pieces of glass, the viewfinder, like the telescopic sight of a sniper rifle.

It was equally strange to see the script we had laboured over being put together with what almost seemed like a comic-strip sensibility. I tracked the designer, the cinematographer, the armourer, the props master, the composer and elicited the oddest statements. Filters the cinematographer was using to replicate the impression of the colour blur that happened at the edges of comic-strip frames. Armour that seemed impos-sibly gleaming, in varieties of silver and gold. These knights had dinner in armour, had their breakfast in armour, even raped their womenfolk in armour. And Camelot, when it was eventually built on a rise above the Dargle river, was a sheer façade of the kind of gleaming silver metal that Frank Gehry would popularize, much, much later. Nothing was as I had imagined it, the kind of mossy, ancient, oaken green world out of which these legends had sprung. I interviewed John about it and he explained his logic – what we see as old now was once new. Tintagel would have been built once, as new and as metallic as the central bank building that was rising above a ruined Temple Bar in central Dublin. I under-stood but didn't feel it. But he did, and it was his *Excalibur*, his film, his imagination. So Merlin wore a cloak like a dragon's cape and a silver, metallic skullcap. Lancelot lay with Guinevere underneath the Powerscourt Waterfall, the sunlight gleaming off his unblemished silver armour. Arthur plunged the sword Excalibur between Lancelot's shimmering breastplate and her naked breast, drawing no blood from either. It was, I finally understood, as I saw John putting it together, a fantasy.

Would the National Film School in Beaconsfield, England, have given me a better education, had I been able to afford it? It might have tutored me more in the niceties of criticism, but I doubt if it could have given me the same sense of the muscularity, the sweat, the effort of one man's mastery over contingency of the real thing. And *Excalibur*, for all of its excesses, was the real thing.

Angel

I was playing in a series of bands at the time to make some extra money. I always had a facility with instruments, particularly stringed ones. Anything with a string: banjo, mandolin, ukulele and the ubiquitous guitar. Although I always had a problem with the guitar; having been trained classically, I regarded that strumming business as kind of Neanderthal crudeness. But I saw a second-hand trumpet in one of those pawn shops in Capel Street and began to attempt to play it, much to the distress of the family dog. I traded it in for a second-hand saxophone and did a little better. So with this band I began to play the brass parts in the middle eights, or choruses. It was remarkably easy: two or three blown riffs would fill out the sound and give the sense at least of a brass section.

I travelled with one or two of these bands, always in a van, bouncing round the back, daytime there, night-time home. The Northern 'Troubles' were in their full glory, but it did seem musicians were immune. So we'd drive to Belfast, Newry, Antrim (never Derry for some reason) and drive back home, always at night. There was the business of the closed-off roads, British army and RUC checkpoints, and then blundering through an unfamiliar landscape to get back on the main road south. One's imagination proved more dangerous than the rather bleak environment of well-tended farmland and occasional village streets emblazoned with Union Jacks.

For some reason one of the principal venues in the South was in a dancehall opposite Portlaoise prison, the high-security jail. Now this dancehall, in the mangled way of those times, was not a purpose-built dancehall. If it had been such, it would probably have been built as a cinema, with a decorative, flat breeze-block frontage, something odd and oriental (and touching, oddly enough) about the castellated way the blocks ascended towards a triangular point, and probably repurposed as a showband dancehall, owned and operated by Albert Reynolds (owner of a string of ballrooms and one day to be Taoiseach). No, this dancehall was part of the mental hospital complex, which sat, grey and institutionally forbidding and Victorian, across the road from the circling klieg lights of the prison itself.

A large, all-purpose hall with a stage which must have served as a recreation room for the patients in the asylum (as these facilities were called then). I was standing alone on the stage, after the sound check, and testing the way the saxophone sounded through the microphone. There was a pleasing echo from the immense space below and I began to happily riff, totally alone, as if I could really play. And, gradually, ghostly figures drifted in from both doors. Dressed in cast-off, ill-fitting clothes with that strange shuffle of the long-time institutionalized. They were prisoners here, I realized, no less incarcerated than the politicals in the klieg-lit Colditz across the road. They shuffled in, as silent as moths, and I kept playing as the walls below me gradually filled. I had a large, utterly voiceless audience immobilized probably by lithium. They seemed to will me to keep on, and I did, until a phalanx of white-coated nurses strode in, clapped their hands and ushered them back out.

Other, more dramatic situations probably inspired the script for my first feature, *Angel*. Journeys back at night in a Southern-registered van after concerts in Belfast; the murders of the Miami Showband on a road outside Newry. There was the idea, simple and horrible, of a saxophone player using his case to hide an Uzi sub-machine gun (and when I came to make the film, one fitted like a glove into the other). But the one that made it peculiarly emblematic of those strange times was that scene in the dancehall-cum-mental hospital in Portlaoise.

I remember nothing of the gig afterwards. (The kids of the town trundling down to the mental hospital for a blast of rock and roll?) But I remember everything about that scene.

I wrote a script which I called *Angel* about a musician who exchanges his saxophone for a gun. The Uzi fits quite neatly into his tenor sax case. It was a bare bones and brutal little parable about the ease with which one could kill someone who otherwise you might have been friends with. A constant refrain in the dialogue was Danny, the anti-hero, requesting the names of those he was about to wreak vengeance upon. I consciously stripped it of all political resonance since I felt the problem in the island I lived in was perhaps the politics, perhaps the religious antagonisms, but most of all the ease with which neighbours could blow each other into eternity.

I showed it to John. It may have been influenced by his *Point Blank*, and the bare allegory of revenge it presented, but what I had written was more complicated, more accidental than that. I wanted a story of murder dressed up as a musical. I had this image of a figure in a shiny, probably pink or gold lamé showband suit wandering with his saxophone case in a forest he didn't understand.

John liked the script and showed it to some of his associates in Los Angeles. They all responded that they would like it better if it were set in an American landscape. Which was, of course, impossible, so things rested there.

Then I happened to be approached by someone from Channel Four. I sent them the script, which they liked, and they asked to meet me in London. I travelled over there, met Walter Donohue, an American, and David Rose, the wise and perspicacious commissioner of film.

I remembered my other experience, the garbled, unrecognizable version of the previous script I had written. The whole process had gone some way towards wrecking my marriage. I loved the flights of imagination this medium took me into, would have been happy to write for it forever, but couldn't face the same experience again.

So when David and Walter began to enquire about directors for the current script, I was bold enough to propose myself. Not only to propose myself, but to let them know that if I didn't direct it, no one else would.

They then, very politely and cautiously, asked about my experience in that regard. I showed them the documentary I had made on the making of *Excalibur*. Not only that, but I told them, quite precipitously and quite boldly, that John had agreed to produce the film. With me as director.

In the subsequent fracas that developed, after the production of *Angel*, I felt a fair amount of guilt. John had, indeed, agreed to produce it, if any financing could be found. When I came back from meeting Channel Four, he was presented with something like a fait accompli. But he very bravely stuck to his word, found matching finance from the Irish Film Board and I, to my surprise and terror, had a feature film on my hands.

There were several problems. The first was that an indigenous feature film hadn't been made in Ireland for a long, long time. Second, I was a writer, not a director. And last that Mr Boorman, despite being resident in the country for twenty years or so and almost single-handedly keeping Ardmore Studios alive, was English and not Irish. (It was a long time ago, when this still mattered.)

Anyway, the news gave rise to the kind of uproar that had ensued when J. M. Synge used the word 'shift' on the stage of the Abbey Theatre. Or when Brendan Behan wrote *Borstal Boy* and became 'the best banned in the land'. Or when John McGahern published *The Dark* and described a policeman's son masturbating into his sock. Or when the same John married a Scandinavian divorcee.

It was odd to be the focus of that kind of controversy. Odder still, to be making a feature film while in the centre of it. It was a small country, I suppose, and there were few opportunities. And I, a mere writer, had fallen into one of them. But the bulk of the financing was coming from Channel Four, so what was the issue? John resigned from the Film Board in the subsequent fracas, so I suppose that became the issue. And I still had a film to make.

Jim Sheridan was working at the Abbey at the same time, stuck in the theatre, which I suppose he resented, but he had mounted a production of a Tom Murphy play called *The Blue Macushla*. It was an odd one, as if a 1930s Warner Brothers gangster saga had been set in Ireland of the seventies. It didn't please everyone. Maybe it was found to be too imagistic, like most of Jim's work, images that needed to break onto a film set, not on a stage. It would be a few years before he brought his genius with actors and emotion to the cinema with *My Left Foot*.

But it starred an actor in a homburg and a gaberdine coat called Stephen Rea.

Stephen was from Belfast. He had been directed by Samuel Beckett, Harold Pinter, Sam Shepard and now by Jim Sheridan. I found his stillness on stage extraordinary. I arranged to meet him, and wanted to see that stillness in person. I gave him the script to read, and we began a journey that still hasn't ended.

He read my script. He played my saxophone. He even wore my coat, when the costume department couldn't find a proper one. I began to understand his relationships with Beckett, Pinter, Shepard. He was at the absolute service of the text, the ideas inside it, and the world it was attempting to convey. Invisible, in a way. He became more invisible with his engagement with Field Day, Brian Friel, Seamus Heaney and Seamus Deane. At the service of Friel's texts, Heaney's, and I often wonder what his trajectory would have been had he followed the usual path. Success in Ireland and Britain, then a career in Hollywood. There were no Samuel Becketts in Hollywood, but there would be, soon, a Sam Shepard.

I cast him as my anti-hero and hired Chris Menges to photograph it. It was an odd and almost terrifying experience, directing a film with a crew that fully expect you to fall on your face and fail. Not only fail, but take the reins, when you collapse in a nervous heap, or are, eventually, fired. Chris understood the script, in fact loved it, and the process and how to deal with the on-set tensions. He came from the English realist tradition, though, and had raised it to a level of poetry with Ken Loach, in *Kes* and *Cathy Come Home*. I had one concept in mind for this film: it was a musical set in a blasted landscape of sectarian violence. I dressed the band Danny, the anti-hero, played in in costumes of glittering gold and pink lamé. I wanted what should have been a neon-tinged fantasy to be overwhelmed by the colours of burned-out buildings and the oiled and smoking barrel of a gun. It is amazing, in retrospect, how far a simple set of images can carry you. I knew nothing about tracking shots and complementary close-ups, was in danger of shooting just the pieces of celluloid I wanted, without any awareness of what might be needed in the editing room. All I knew was what I wanted to see. Chris, who came from the social-realist world of things, wanted to situate the violence of the film with a broader social sense of things. Riots on Belfast streets, British army violent responses to the same. I refused. I wanted the cycle of violence the Uzi led the central character towards to be nothing but an existential fact in itself. He killed people he would have otherwise befriended. Before he pulled the trigger, he asked them their name. This was to be an allegory, not a documentary. A Grimms' tale gone wrong. Chris responded to the contrasts of gold lamé intensity and dull burned-out greens with a fairy-tale magic and a sense of theatricality that would become the film. Maybe we were both learning.

Angel, *Bray Promenade.*

So, I had finished this strange thing, a film, and was exhausted by both the experience and the controversy surrounding it. John Boorman must have been as exhausted. The public outcry over the allocation of funds from the Irish Film Board had disgusted him so much that he resigned. The bulk of the funding, after all, had come from Channel Four. The resulting arguments would continue for years. He had watched me edit this fairy-tale-cum-musical-cum-revenge saga, seen me go in directions he would never have gone himself, but let me at it. And we now had to bring it to London to show it to the directors of Film on Four. I fully expected to be burned at the stake for the scandalous waste of their resources. After the screening Jeremy Isaacs, the director of the channel, began a slow handclap. He took us to a pub called the Intrepid Fox and told me the film justified the whole enterprise of Film on Four. It was for films like this he set it up.

London

It seems paradoxical, or counter-intuitive, or just plain weird, but the thing I remember about London in the late seventies and early eighties was the warmth of the reception a young Irish emigrant/refugee received. This was a London without the need for illegal squats, casual labour and street sleeping. And this in the worst period of the IRA bombing campaign, the days of the unrelenting Margaret Thatcher. But it was as if a different person had arrived on those shores, from a plane this time, not a boat and train. No more Holyhead and Euston Green.

I was awarded the *Guardian* Fiction Prize along with a Zimbabwean writer, Dambudzo Marechera. My book was called *Night in Tunisia*, his was called *The House of Hunger*. The reception was held in the huge, mirrored lobby of the Theatre Royal, Drury Lane. I wore a maroon double-breasted jacket with a stripe, Dambudzo wore a coloured poncho and a cowboy hat. I suppose the phrase 'the great and the good' would apply to those who were there, but there was an almost willed understatement to their dress and their demeanour and a diffidence that I hadn't encountered before, a resistance to any sense of display that I would later come to see as quint-essentially English. Dambudzo was all display: his cowboy boots, his Mexican or Zimbabwean poncho, his cigarettes and his cowboy hat. Angela Carter made a short speech, Bill Webb, the *Guardian* literary editor, made another, and some kind of plaque, or scroll, or maybe even a cheque was handed over to me, and then to Dambudzo. Did I make a speech? I must have. Because, after me, Dambudzo spoke. And then the fireworks started.

He talked about the stench of colonial patronage coming off the very idea of the award. About the similar sense of colo-nial patronage he had experienced at New College, Oxford. The audience nodded in assent; they appreciated this critique of their culture, which they themselves undoubtedly shared. But this civilized acceptance only seemed to drive Dambudzo to a greater sense of outrage. His voice rose. He grabbed a tray from a passing waiter, scattering the champagne flutes, and threw it at one of the gilt mirrors.

Now these were large gold-embossed mirrors, tall enough to display the whole gathering, as the silver tray spun towards their reflected faces, bounced off it, leaving little more than a crack. What amazed me was the response more than the violence of the event itself. A slight murmur of embarrassment, which could have even been misinterpreted as approval. Which seemed to drive Dambudzo to an even greater fury. He strode off the little dais we had been perched on, and grabbed one of those high-backed, satin-covered chairs. Threw that at a different mirror. Then repeated the process.

One often feels that way, doesn't one, someone said to me. Was it Carmen Callil or Angela Carter or Ursula Owen, or Bill Webb?

But one rarely acts it.

Dambudzo was certainly acting it, with three or four friends now, who were either attempting to restrain him or join in the mayhem. Eventually he was subdued by security – again quite politely, and escorted outside.

It was my first experience of that quintessentially English response to manufactured chaos and outrage against their institutions. Embarrassment.

I met Dambudzo outside, after the revels had ended. He was sitting on the street, like an émigré from the High Andes, in his poncho and his black cowboy hat. He had nowhere to stay. I took him back, to whatever spare room I was inhabiting. Tim O'Grady's, I seem to remember, a friend of mine. He slept on the carpet, underneath my bed. There was a bottle of whiskey involved, which was still half full beside him when he woke. He began drinking it before I had brewed the tea. Talked more about his plight – and seemed to find Mugabe an even greater potential oppressor than the foyer of the Theatre Royal, the patronage of the *Guardian* and colonial Britain. Thought he might join me in Ireland, in post-colonial splendour. I couldn't imagine him in Dublin, even less in the West of Ireland. Had the kind of display that I'd witnessed happened in the Gaiety or Abbey Theatre, he would have spent two or three bruised nights in Mountjoy. I told him things were rougher over there, and he might find the experience even more disenchanting. Then he finished the whiskey and walked into the Shepherd's Bush dawn.

Neil Jordan and Dambudzo Marechera,
Guardian *Fiction Prize.*

I did love London then. It was the sum of all contradictions.

My next experience of cultural – or colonial? – misunder-standing was in the Royal Albert Hall. My first film, *Angel*, had been released in Stephen Woolley's Scala Cinema. I was there to do some publicity with Honor Heffernan and Stephen Rea, who starred in the film. Honor, being a jazz singer, had been invited to partake in a medley of Beatles tunes that were being performed in front of Paul McCartney and the royal family, at the Albert Hall. I walked in with a shoulder bag, which contained the manuscript of a novel I was writing at the time, into that splendid circular interior where one of those dreadful orchestral versions of 'Eleanor Rigby' or 'Hey Jude' was playing. Honor was due to sing 'The Long and Winding Road' just before the interval. I thought I should wish her well, backstage. I blundered from my seat, made my way backstage, wished her the best and was making my way back upstairs when, from several different directions, all at once, I was surrounded by a group of very well dressed and well-spoken males. They surrounded me, like a bevy of polite and insistent courtiers, and ushered me outside where my shoulder bag was sitting on the pavement, surrounded by klieg lights and police vehicles, with one of those remote-controlled bomb-detonation devices being lifted out of an open van.

There were hands on my elbow but there wasn't a hint of violence. I wasn't thrown to the ground, wrists twisted behind my back and handcuffed. Instead I was asked, with that clipped, rather deadly courtesy, if the bag was mine. I said it was and wondered how it had made the transition from underneath my seat to this busy throughfare called, I noticed from the street sign, Kensington Gore. What an extraordinary name, I thought, as I was asked again would I very much mind opening my bag. It was a Royal Command performance, I was reminded, the Queen and Prince Philip were in attendance, along with other members of the royal family. And I finally understood. How stupid of me. I apologized, and walked, under the glare of police headlights, and opened my bag. Showed the offices the pile of unoffending papers. And was escorted back up the steps towards the Albert Hall.

Then I got my first experience of celebrity.

An explosion, of flashbulbs from the massed paparazzi, and some of them still had flash bulbs then. A round of shouted questions, what's in the case? Repeated then, with a suffix. Tell us what's in the case, Paddy? I wasn't a celebrity now, I was back to being a Paddy. I tried to duck round the vaulted entrances back into the auditorium but was followed by a gentleman from the William Hickey column of the *Daily Express* who wanted to know what was inside the bag that had caused so much trouble on Kensington Gore. A novel, I told him, as he followed me inside. He was handsome and impeccable in his dress suit, but wouldn't let me go. What kind of novel, when would it be published. So this is what fame is like, I remember thinking, I could give him the name (*The Past*) and the publisher (Jonathan Cape) and maybe even increase the sales. But I squeezed past him and back into my seat, tried to ignore the disapproving glances and heard the London Symphony Orchestra begin the first few bars of 'The Long and Winding Road'.

He is far too persistent, that journalist, I remember thinking, and too polite. I got a phone call, several days later in whatever office or hotel I happened to be in, and was told that the same journalist from the *Daily Express* was on the line. He wanted more of the story, more details of the novel, what did I do when I got back in, how was the concert, the party afterwards. There was no party, I just went home, I told him, wondering how he got my number. This was well before the days of mobile phones. Several phone calls later, I began to worry for him. This obsession seemed unhealthy.

And several days later again, there was an actual explosive device, with a warning call from the IRA, placed at Harrods.

As the store was being evacuated and the streets were actually, with necessity and urgency, being cordoned off, that young journalist pushed his way through the crush to get a better story and was killed when the bomb exploded.

Stanley

I was living in a house in Bray at the time with my two daughters when I thought I'd go for a walk. It was a safe environment for two young girls, the main danger being the waves that would pound the promenade, usually to their great excitement. I could send the youngest, Anna, down to the amusements at the rattier end of the promenade with a few coins in the daytime with her friends, in full confidence that they would return safely and that she would have multiplied the coins, since she had worked out some mysterious combination on the plastic horses that jerked along for a few pennies. I don't remember if the waves were high that night, but they probably were since it was mid-October. Anyway, when I returned home Sarah, the eldest, told me someone had called. English, she thought, probably from the film business, since that was what was drawing me across the water at the time. Stanley Cooper was his name, she thought, and he had left a number. I didn't know any Stanley Cooper, so I put off the return call until the next day and forgot all about it. Then the next night she told me the same Mr Cooper had called again. So I called back the number he had left and found myself talking, not to a production manager or a journalist called Cooper but to Stanley Kubrick. He had seen *Angel*, and was kind enough to be intrigued. By the fact that I was a novelist, and now a film-maker, and wanted to talk.

Several days later, another call. I was reading Walter Benjamin at the time and was fascinated by his reading of a story by Herodotus, on the captured Egyptian king who refused to weep until he saw his servant paraded in front of him, in chains. How the story that refuses explanation has the most power. I was amazed he didn't seem to have read, or heard of, Benjamin, neither him, nor the essay, 'The Work of Art in the Age of Mechanical Reproduction'.

Several days later, yet another call. Another conversation. I began to understand that this man's entry into most areas of intellectual curiosity was through images, in particular moving ones. With most of us it is the other way around. What a fascinating, almost painstaking way to approach reality, let alone the world. He concluded this call by asking if I ever came to London to have dinner with him.

Several days later I was going to London and called him. He gave me the name and address of a restaurant, in Chelsea as far as I remember, and very precise instructions as to the front entrance, which he described in detail. When I open the front door, he told me, there will be a staircase facing me, heading downwards. Once down below, there would be a table to the left, from which all of the traffic up and down the restaurant could be observed. He would book that table for eight o clock.

I flew to London and had a meeting with Stephen Woolley, who had released my movie *Angel*. I told him I had to meet Mr Kubrick the next evening, which excited him exorbitantly. He had a cinema, called the Scala. He begged me to ask Stanley about a possible rerelease of *A Clockwork Orange*. I knew there had been some scandal about the film, but didn't know the details, and promised I would.

The next evening I made my way to the restaurant, where exactly in Chelsea, I can't remember now. But I can remember the front entrance. Stanley's description of it was so exact, it was almost like a remembered dream. I opened the door, and, sure enough, facing me was a small staircase, leading downwards. Before I could take the first step, a maître d' type came towards me and without asking my name led me down the staircase. To a table, to the left, facing all of the traffic up and down the stairs. I took my seat and waited, watching the swinging front door, as various besuited great ones came and went. Which of them, I wondered, would turn out to be my host, when down the stairs came a tousled figure in a green combat jacket, pockets stuffed with notepads, who introduced himself as Stanley Kubrick.

He sat, we ordered food and began to talk. And the extraordinary thing was that he seemed to remember everything from our phone conversations. After two hours of this, and maybe a coffee, I felt it would be polite not to waste any more of the great man's time, and hinted I might leave. But no, he said, and I don't think he referred to a notebook, we still haven't talked about what we discussed on 24 October. I had no idea what we talked about on 24 October but he did, even down to chapter and verse of whatever books and movies we had discussed. The feat of memory amazed me, and I thought I must be talking to some kind of unique intelligence or someone who recorded all his phone calls and had developed a habit of listening back to them. And over the course of an acquaintance that would last another few years I came to realize that both were probably true.

In fact the only way to end the evening was the request from Mr Woolley about a possible rerelease of *A Clockwork Orange*. He wanted to talk about everything but that. It had caused him the kind of trouble he didn't want to repeat.

The Company of Wolves

Stephen Woolley, who had a company called Palace Pictures which was financed by Nik Powell, who was once Richard Branson's partner and who was married to Sandie Shaw – and that is an awful lot of 'whos', I know – was a great supporter of *Angel*. The film was released in several cinemas and he told me he was anxious to move from distribution into production. Stephen had that extraordinary punk enthusiasm of the time, was one of the earliest fans of the Sex Pistols, a north Londoner who supported Tottenham Hotspur and had an immense love and knowledge of cinema, but knew nothing of the agonies of production. I knew enough to realize how painful it all could be. He told me he wanted to commission a script from me, so I went back to Dublin, Bray, where I was living at the time, a newly separated father of two with a complicated relationship with their mother. She did me the great grace and favour, though, of allowing me to share their upbringing. So they would come out to this Victorian pile I lived in by the sea and spend half the week with me. The fabled Christmas dinner of the Joyces, so memorably described in *A Portrait of the Artist as a Young Man* (has there ever been a worse title for a better book?) had taken place in the house next door. The Joyces had lived there before their father's alcoholism took them to the Northside, around Lower Drumcondra, where, Joyce would claim, the best English was spoken. My twin uncles still ran the chemist's shop on Main Street where Eileen Vance once lived, who broke young James Joyce's childhood heart. I was living there and writing and trying to imagine a script I could write for Mr Woolley, when an event took place in Dublin, celebrating the 100th anniversary of Joyce's birth. Writers came to Dublin from all around the planet, Jorge Luis Borges, Anthony Burgess, Dennis Potter and Angela Carter among them. I was introduced to Borges, who went all onomastic with my name – 'Neil, from the Icelandic Njal?'

'No,' I told him, 'from the Irish Niall.'

I had a brief acquaintance with Angela from the mirror-smashing ceremony at the *Guardian* Fiction Prize and we got talking. She cut a wicked, dramatic figure in Dublin with her bluestocking dresses and her long grey hair. She gave me a short radio play she had written, based on her short story 'The Company of Wolves'. It was too short to develop into a script for a movie but I read again her entire collection, *The Bloody Chamber*, and came up with an idea. Two films I loved – *The Saragossa Manuscript* and *Valerie and Her Week of Wonders* – could maybe provide a template for us. *The Saragossa Manuscript* had this delightful structure of stories within stories, often initiated by characters within the cinematic fictions themselves. *Valerie and Her Week of Wonders* was a fantasy about a young girl's movement into puberty. If we used the 'Saragossa' method of tales within tales within tales, of storytellers within a fiction maybe telling us other fictions, we could perhaps find a way of embracing other stories within *The Bloody Chamber*, all within the context of a young girl's experience of puberty. Menstrual blood in a horror compendium. A werewolf saga about a young girl's sexuality. *The Saragossa Manuscript* meets *The Wolfman* meets *Valerie and Her Week of Wonders*. I can imagine the pitch, in a Hollywood studio I was yet to encounter. I can imagine the bemused smiles, the shaking heads.

Stephen Woolley had yet to encounter Hollywood, though, and was enthusiastic. His company would pay for a script to be written if Angela agreed. And Angela, with her love of cinema and transgressive narratives, actually did agree. So I made my way back to London and began the trip every morning from a Soho hotel to Clapham Common, where she lived with her tiny baby and her husband Mark, whom she occasionally called 'The Wolf'. He did have wild hair, a West Country accent and could have stepped from a scene in *Straw Dogs*. We worked in her office in the basement, while he wrestled with a pottery wheel and looked after the infant somewhere above.

We established an alarmingly simple way of working. We would talk about what we would write in the morning, outline scenes together, and then go our separate ways for the rest of the day and write them. We would meet the next morning, compare drafts and begin the whole process again. There would be a dream within a dream, a granny within that dream, who would tell stories to a young Rosaleen, who would meet other characters within these stories and the process would begin again. Each tale would contain a lesson, a cautionary one, as in most fairy tales. And we established one critical principal. If an image or a set of images crept into the structure, unbidden, without any connection to the above structure, we would welcome it. Hence a bird's nest with tiny eggs that crack, revealing tiny Buddhas. Hence a rose that turns red under a wolf girl's tears. A grandmother's severed head breaks into pieces like a childhood toy.

We had the script finished in about two weeks, and I gave it to Stephen Woolley, who was intrigued. But he wondered how to finance it. I gave it to Walter Donohue and David Rose of Channel Four, who were anxious to see what I would come up with after *Angel*. But they found it too fantastical. They said I was straying too far from my forte, which they termed as 'poetic realism'. And maybe they were right, but I hadn't known until then that I was a poetic realist. Then Stephen found a partner in a very old, traditional manager of a British film company called ITC. This elderly gentleman loved the script and put up a small enough sum, around two million, for us to begin this extravagant fantasy.

Terry Gilliam had just made *Brazil*, which cut new swathes into design and visual effects, so I first approached his designer, who turned it down. Then I met an extravagant and untried genius, Anton Furst, who had designed a small movie for Chris Petit, *An Unsuitable Job for a Woman*, and had done some effects work on Ridley Scott's *Alien*.

Anton loved the script and began to draw. He began amassing images of expressionistic Germanic forests. I introduced him to Samuel Palmer's hallucinatory paintings of English villages. We pored over books of Piranesi etchings and Gustave Doré's engravings and the images grew, like untameable undergrowth. A tree could be anything, we decided. It could have bark like stripped human musculature, twigs could become like splayed fingers, the roots could shape themselves into a fairy-tale house or a high-heeled shoe. Or an abandoned, twisted organ. At the one end of this forest, or the centre? – it was already defying geography and geometry – was to be a Samuel Palmer bridge with a village behind, a church steeple that bent slightly, either with age or as if made of some ancient wax. At the centre of this village was to be a well with a Heath Robinson mechanism that allowed a hooked bucket to descend into the depths of the earth, which thankfully we would never see, since we couldn't afford it. This bucket would at one stage raise a wolf girl into the moonlit village. The moon itself would be a backlit circle of lace. This moon would weep, if we could manage it, tears of blood. For a vista over the wider forest, when the young heroine Rosaleen climbed the highest tree, we would use bonsai trees to create the illusion of a horizon. There would be mushrooms, bigger than humans, giant teddy bears, wedding banquets and wolves. So many wolves.

We could afford two stages in the old Shepperton Studios and if we used the doors between them as a kind of wooded bower, we could set the village in one stage and the forest in another. So Anton began to build, but ran out of money for the forest. His solution was ingenious. He could afford, at most, twelve giant trees and had the idea of placing them on rollers, so they could be wheeled, to create a different angle and another forest vista. We would create rainbows with glass paintings, manipulate those trees so the forest could change from winter to summer, within the same tracking shot. Wild, wonderful and stupidly ambitious.

Christopher Tucker joined us, a genius of prosthetic makeup who had designed *The Elephant Man*. I went through the wolf transformations with him. It was to be a werewolf movie, after all, hidden inside a fairy tale. The problem, he explained to me, was basically one of geometry. Changing the flat profile of a human into the V-shaped profile of your average wolf. A mechanical structure that stretched one into the other, even if we could build a prosthetic human face, was impossible. So we came up with different scenarios. In one, the human actor would tear his skin off, to gradually reveal the wolf inside. It had a pleasing allegoric sheen to it. Every man was to conceal a wolf, after all, particularly one whose eyebrows meet in the middle. The same wolf had to return to his household, see his abandoned wife with another husband and turn back into a man. I came up with the idea of the terrified wife severing his wolf head with an axe, which tumbles into a vat of milk and sinks. It rises to the surface with the visage of the husband she once loved.

So that was two down.

The third was the most complicated. Rosaleen meets a huntsman in the winter forest. The huntsman has a pleasing Old World grace to him, and seems to have stepped straight out of the pages of Heinrich von Kleist. He walks her back home through the forest to her grandmother's cabin, but the grandmother, of course, is searching the wintry forests for her. And once inside the cabin a seduction begins, which leads to the grandmother's decapitation by a blast of a shotgun from Rosaleen, and the wounded huntsman's transformation into yet another wolf.

I suppose the basic scenario gave us a clue. The huntsman, played with a muscular beauty by the dancer Micha Bergese, would recoil from the wound. What if his skin split to reveal the furred creature underneath? He would howl in agony. What if a wolf pushed through his howling open mouth? We began to draw and an image emerged – the magical transformation of the flat profile of a human into the V-shaped profile of a wolf. One pushing through the other's mouth.

So that was three down.

The forest was finished and a crew was hired, and each one of them, it seemed, had walked straight from the Pinewood set of *The Empire Strikes Back*. It's hard to describe, in these days of inclusivity and BAME policies, the contempt with which these crews treated the whole enterprise. If you want to lay the tracks there, guvnor, it's your funeral. I was a young Irish ingenue, I suppose, dealing with illusions and imponderables that bewildered these practical sappers. They had worked on Bond movies, after all. But then Chris Menges, who had shot *Angel* for me, had shot second unit on *The Empire Strikes Back* and told me they treated George Lucas with the same contempt. So I did what one has to do: drew those few crew members close who seemed to understand the enterprise. Brian Loftus, the cinematographer. Mike Roberts, the operator. Peter MacDonald, the second unit director. And most of all, the actors.

They understood. Angela Lansbury played a fairy-tale granny with all of the wit she had brought to *Bedknobs and Broomsticks* and *Sweeney Todd*. David Warner, Terence Stamp, Sarah Patterson, Micha Bergese, Tusse Silberg, Stephen Rea, Danielle Dax.

We finished the film anyway, with a beautiful score by George Fenton, and Stephen Woolley decided to open it in the Odeon Leicester Square. That was the biggest cinema in England at the time with more than two thousand seats, and screening it there was regarded as an even more foolhardy gamble than the film itself. There was one of those glamorous openings with microphones in front of the huge screen, an introduction from me facing what seemed like two thousand sceptical critics, just barely withholding their wintry judgements.

But it seemed to go well and I remember walking back up Charing Cross Road with Stephen afterwards. Crowds were lining the pavement all the way from Leicester Square back to Soho and I asked Stephen what were they queueing for?

Your movie, you idiot. The late-night screening.

It was a strange world, this film-making business. The film created quite the stir in England, a bigger one back in Ireland. It made waves in France and Spain and even Japan, and eventually it made its way to the US, where it was released by Menahem Golan and Yoram Globus and Cannon Pictures as a straight-up horror movie. Now I had put horror elements deliberately into the film. There was a surfeit of beheadings, leaping and snarling wolves, there was even the spectacle of Stephen Rea tearing his own skin off and a wolf-mouth pushing its way through Micha Bergese's open lips. They made a poster, with the tagline 'In the dead of night, the beast is unleashed!' They made a trailer, promising a bloodfest.

I was in New York for the opening and Chris Brown, one of the producers, hired a limo to visit some of the cinemas screening it, one in Times Square but the majority spread through the upper reaches of Manhattan.

Most of the cinema ushers were armed.

Chris would politely ask them what the evening attendance was like. They would reply with shrugs, scowls, sometimes no answer at all, or the reply, Who the fuck are you?

One of them, unarmed, said she'd go down to call the manager. Another usher pulled her back, said hang on, and called an armed guard.

'That's how Billy got it last week.'

We ended up at a midnight screening in Times Square, where outraged clients, expecting to see the bloodfest the trailer promised, were treated to a fairy tale.

'Fuck this thing. It's Little Red Riding Hood!'

I kept quiet about my authorship.

My Friends

I got another call from Stanley.

Your friends did another number last night.

They're not my friends, Stanley.

He meant the IRA. I had sent him an early draft of the script of a film I wanted to make, *Michael Collins*. He had been kind enough to read and respond to it, so maybe I was now guilty by association. But he had a different reason for calling. A friend of his, a 'multi-multi-millionaire', wanted to buy a house by the sea.

You live by the sea, don't you?

I told him I did.

Well, this friend had very specific instructions as to the kind of property he needed. It had to be on a promontory, overlooked by nobody, and approachable by only one road from the land. He described the imagined place in detail. I could see it, but couldn't help wondering who this friend was.

Someone very well known, with a great hatred of publicity.

That reminds me of someone, I couldn't help thinking but didn't say.

What I did say was that Ireland was the kind of place that tended to leave people alone. In fact I knew one of them, and could put him in touch, if he wanted.

Who?

The lead singer of a band called U2.

U2? They're a band?

A very popular one.

And what's his name?

Bono.

Bono? Is that a name?

His name. Or what he calls himself.

He calls himself Bono? Just Bono?

He has another name, if you want it.

No, he said. Just find out would he take a call from me.

I found out. Bono lived in a Martello Tower above me in Bray. We met in the Harbour Bar. He would be more than happy to talk to Mr Kubrick.

This all was before email and text. Everything had to be a letter, a meeting or a phone call. And at the time, tax-free exemption for artists had been introduced by the Taoiseach, Charlie Haughey.

So maybe this friend was an artist of some kind. And I called Stanley back. Gave him the number, and eventually after a day or two he responded.

I'm not going to call your friend Bono.

No?

No. Because the friend is actually me. And I know all he'll tell me is I'm being paranoid. And I don't want to hear that from someone I don't know.

But he invited me to visit him in his house in St Albans.

I would get the train to St Albans and Mr Kubrick would be there in a Mini Cooper and drive me to the grey-coloured mansion in the grounds where he lived. So isolated and bucolic, I had to wonder why he ever thought of moving to Ireland. We would have takeaway food and brandy, and he would bum the cigarettes that I smoked. He told me about his plans for his movie on Napoleon. Told me he had finally decided on the title of his next one, *Full Metal Jacket*. A ballistics description, of a certain kind of bullet casing. He gave me a Christmas present, of a set of reproductions of Canaletto whom he thought of as the best matte artist that ever lived. He told me the only reason for living in Los Angeles was the money and the pretty girls, and he had no need for either.

He hired the designer of *The Company of Wolves*, Anton Furst, to construct Hué, Vietnam, at Beckton Gasworks, London. Anton was hired, after *Full Metal Jacket*, by Tim Burton to design *Batman* and won an Oscar for it. Los Angeles and fame did a number on him, which may account for his jump off the roof of the Cedars-Sinai Medical Center onto the pavement of Beverly Boulevard, below. Someone told me people commit suicide as an act of revenge against the people or the places that have driven them to that point. If that was truly the case, Stanley Kubrick had a point about Los Angeles.

Movies I Haven't Made 1

*L*ucky Stars
        When *The Company of Wolves* played in the Savoy
Cinema in Dublin, it was given an 18 certificate. So my daughters couldn't attend. Neither, apparently, could blind people
with guide dogs. I didn't know blind people attended the
cinema, but apparently they did, enjoyed the immersive aural
experience and often had the visuals explained to them by
their carers or partners. But canines were excluded. So neither
wolves nor young girls could watch my film.

I would have loved to make a film that my daughters could
watch, whatever about their dog, Rickie. It would have had to
be in rhyming couplets because of a game we played before
they went to sleep. I would invent a few lines of doggerel and
they would have to finish the rhyme.

> *Little Maisie was so very bold*
> *She would never finish her dinner*
> *She watched it go gooey and cold*
> *And so she grew...*
> *Thinner and thinner!*

We would watch a lot of Shirley Temple and Judy Garland movies. *Meet Me in St Louis, Rebecca of Sunnybrook Farm*, before John Hughes, *Pretty in Pink* and Molly Ringwald took their adolescent attention. All on the large television on the pink sofa in the room overlooking Bray Head.

I made up a story which they begged me to turn into a movie so I wrote the script. About a child star in some whizz-bang Flash Gordon future, trawling the universe searching for her lost father, who was a comedian last seen entertaining intergalactic troops, trying to reconquer a lost planet ruled by runaway toys.

The father must have been me, the universe Hollywood, the child star either one of them.

I wrote Busby Berkeley numbers involving the tap-dancing heroine in a spaceship full of decommissioned robot parts, one of them with musical abilities. Called Mozart, of course.

I invented an intergalactic tour bus with space travelling hoofers with hearts of gold.

A malignant mustachioed manager chasing them round planet after planer. Called, for some reason, Rostropovich.

He, like everyone, spoke in rhyming couplets:

I recognize this ribbon from a pretty little head
It's a polka-dotted pattern in her favourite colour red

I even wrote songs for malignant giant toys, based on a Dublin murder ballads, like 'The Night before Larry Was Stretched':

The night the toys took their revenge
The children asleep in the beds were
Their parents, drugged or deranged

At least those that had taken their meds were...
Oh dolly what's that in your hand
It looks very much like a knife?
Oh teddy bear why do you stand
As if you had taken a life?
For Mummy lies dead in her bed
And Daddy's been drowned in the toilet...

It's still in my desk, somewhere.

Mona Lisa

Bob Hoskins was London, in a way. He had been having a great moment, or a series of great moments. I had come across him first in Dennis Potter's beautiful, strange musical thing, *Pennies From Heaven*. He had played the manager in *The Cotton Club*, and turned London into an abattoir in *The Long Good Friday*. I had been working with David Leland on a script that I wanted to call *Mona Lisa*. A released con who became a driver for a hooker, both searching for a lost girl. David had written a script heavily influenced by Paul Schrader's movie *Hardcore*. A father, looking for a daughter, lost in an underworld of porn. David's script was harsh and unrelenting, and there was some talk of Sean Connery playing the central role. An ageing, towering bundle of muscle released from a long sentence, wreaking vengeance on a city he no longer recognizes. Kind of thing. But for some reason it wasn't convincing, either the casting or the central character, and here I was walking through the streets of Islington, looking for a character called George.

I knocked on one of those Victorian Islington brass knockers and the door opened and there was George. Smaller than me, which was unusual enough, with a half-bald, half-shaven bullet head and a pair of braces running over a torso that I seemed to recognize from any number of building sites. I could have been looking at the vinyl salesman from *Pennies From Heaven*, but I was looking at Bob Hoskins.

Come in, mate.

He made me a cup of tea. The accent seemed almost a cliché, of a London from any number of cop shows, but he was the real thing, and my most immediate impression was of one of those Russian dolls, which you unscrew the top of to find a smaller, more compact version, and so ad infinitum. There was something hidden beneath the tough exterior, the north London argot, some huge reservoir of emotion that if unscrewed would lead to another reservoir beneath.

He wasn't hot on the script. I agreed, but felt a twinge of betrayal. David had done a good job, but it was too violent, too unrelenting. Unrelenting violence was a thing at the time, as evidenced by Bob himself in *The Long Good Friday*. But I could immediately see a different story and here, in front of me, a different character. I said give me a week or two, and went off to write.

It was fascinating, moulding a script around an actual actor. This small, rotund character emerged, again, like a Russian doll, full of lost hope and longing. He didn't understand women and never would. But he wanted to, so much. He was divorced, estranged from his wife and daughter, had a huge and mostly restrained capacity for violence. Having served an unspecified number of years inside, he had no compunction about expressing the kind of casual racism a previous genera-tion would have taken for granted. He is given a job by his former boss, Mortwell, for having loyally served his time. The problem being the job is driving what he calls 'a tall, thin black tart' from one assignation to another.

He falls for her, of course, and she is blessed with the kind of sophistication that has totally passed him by. She teaches him to dress better, behave better, and draws him into her own damaged world. She is searching for a girl, who has been taken from her by her former pimp. She asks him to help her. This is a task George can too easily understand, a knight in shining armour in his mustard-coloured Jag, prowling those mean streets and alleyways for a virgin waiting for redemption.

The whole scenario could have led to any number of interpretations, but with the image of Hoskins in my mind the character came alive and drove the show. I gave him a friend, who lives in a caravan near the river, who is obsessed with dime detective novels, and whose current obsession is a little-known work by John Franklin Bardin called *The Deadly Percheron*. I had them explain the plot to each other, in terms that could have developed into their own detective novel. I had them talk in long diversions, with the kind of dialogue that normally would have found itself nowhere near a thriller. I had Mortwell, his criminal boss, run a dancing troupe of strippers and expound on his process like a London Cecil B. DeMille. But most of all I had this character George, who would never, despite his best efforts, understand women. They had to be damsels in distress, virgins in need of rescuing from a swamp, and any contact with the actual reality would have inevitable and tragic results.

Bob liked the script, so much that he thought he had written it. He came on board, and we had, it seemed, a movie. The only problem was that the enterprise of Palace Pictures was almost entirely devoted to a much, much bigger project, *Absolute Beginners*, to be directed by Julien Temple. They were building an enormous set in one of the London studios, and it was to feature every celebrity from the current music scene, including David Bowie. A huge and costly enterprise, covered daily by the tabloids.

It is hard to understand now, but every movie at the time held the future of 'The British Film Industry' on its shoulders. *Chariots of Fire* had won a bunch of Oscars, the writer had proclaimed 'The British are coming' and each new enterprise promised a return to the fabled days of – when? Nobody could be certain, but each new film had two burdens on its shoulders: burden number one, to return British cinema to its great days. Burden number two, to make a searing indictment of Thatcher's Britain. How one could perform both tasks at the same time was a problem. Searing Indictments and a Great Return? There was something contradictory here, but those two burdens fell on the willing shoulders of Stephen and Julien.

Mona Lisa was a smaller movie, and ended up being financed by George Harrison's company, Handmade Films, produced on Stephen's behalf by Patrick Cassavetti. George was a delight but the manager of his company, Dennis O'Brien, was an American and was busy learning all of the worst lessons of a Hollywood executive.

The first confrontation, as always, was the script. Why does George, the Hoskins character, come out of prison? I told him I don't know, and it doesn't really matter, does it? Aha, came the retort, but he owes a favour to his old boss, Mortwell, doesn't he? Surely we have to know why that favour is owed?

It's a red herring, I retorted, doesn't really matter. And if you insist, I'll have him pull up at a fish shop, buy a red herring and deliver it in person to Mortwell. He'll know what it means.

There's only one problem. Herrings aren't red.

My God, you are right, sir. They are generally a fishy coloured grey or silver. OK, I'll have him pull up at a pet store, and buy a white rabbit. He'll give that to Mortwell's messenger boy, and say give that to your boss. He'll know what that means.

There was another kink of fate in my favour. Handmade Films, in their efforts to crack the great American market, were making a film with the newlyweds Sean Penn and Madonna called *Shanghai Surprise*. Again, that promised a return. To the great days of Anna May Wong, Marlene Dietrich and Josef von Sternberg maybe.

Two returns, maybe, allowed me to slip through the cracks.

But that thought of the rabbit was a good one. I wrote the scene, and the white rabbit became its own little sub-motif, straight out of *Alice in Wonderland*, a little like *The Deadly Percheron*. I could have it sit on Mortwell's lap during the final confrontation in Brighton, hop around his bloodied body, reddening its pure white fur.

Anyway, everyone else was busy and George Harrison turned out to be everything you hoped George Harrison would be. It was strange, sitting in a restaurant with one of the Beatles while another walked by, Ringo, and dropped something onto his napkin. A lump of hash, I presumed, which George promptly stuck in his top pocket. He asked me did I remember Bert Weedon. Of course I did, as did anybody who learned guitar in the sixties.

Bert Weedon's *Play in a Day*. It was the only instruction they ever had, he told me, all they needed was three chords, with the occasional minor and, every now and then, the discordant diminished seventh. Stranger still to realize that the entire Beatles catalogue came out of this one book.

So, with George's backing, we made our little movie. His only note was a request that nudity be kept to a minimum. It was unfortunate that the first day's shooting involved Bob Hoskins walking through a steam room, wrapped only in a towel, sinking into a pool to hide himself. We used a splash camera to get an underwater shot which exposed nothing but dangling genitalia and bubbling water. I don't think anyone had seen as many penises on screen outside of a porn movie, at the first day's rushes. Mr Harrison was polite enough to wonder which one of them was Mr Hoskins's.

Sunglasses and Bob Hoskins.

It was a more easily approachable enterprise than *The Company of Wolves*, the main problem being how to turn this suburban London into its own dark forest. There was an industrial, hellish grandeur to some areas of King's Cross. There was the shabby, neon warren that was Soho at the time. There was Raymond Revue bar, with its strange, cantilevered passageway above two streets. I had always wanted to photograph that from above, and from below. And it turned out to be fun, to turn this city into something it was not.

I met Cathy Tyson, a beautiful, extraordinary talent. Michael Caine found a gap between two films and came onboard. I used rehearsal between them both quite selfishly, not so much to prepare the performances as to explore the characters. There were points at which the emotion between them seemed about to reach boiling point, but the script didn't quite get to that point. I'd go off, rewrite the scenes, and hear them read the next day. Using rehearsal as a writing tool proved perfect, for me and I hope for them. The final emotional encounter between George and Simone needed something as old-fashioned as a speech. A kind of cry from the naive male heart of what George had hoped for from the relationship. It was to be set in Brighton, the Brighton of *Brighton Rock*, Donald McGill postcards, candyfloss and dodgem cars. I wanted George to place cheap pink heart-shaped glasses on Simone, talk about how he imagined a walk on that promenade would have been like in some mythical past where a bloke walks with his bird, takes her arm, buys her candyfloss, maybe even dances and kisses her when he hears carnival music. How it was between 'men and fucking women'. He has just learned he has tracked down not her lost sibling but her lover. So I wrote such a speech, heard them both rehearse it in the rehearsal room in Soho, but had no idea how it would play in the film. A film that had become, by now, one about how deeply a man can misunderstand a woman. George had to break hearts here, when he knew he couldn't break Simone's.

We began shooting and it was, strangely enough, a delight. Cathy, who had never shot a film before, had so little awareness of the camera that in the shot in a scene where she storms out of a hotel room onto the streets outside, I turned round after the first take and wondered where she had gone. I had to wander the hotel rooms searching for her, wondered had I offended her, then saw her outside where the taxis line up.

What are you doing out here, I asked her.

Playing the scene, she said. He follows me out, gets in the car, says sorry and off we go again.

But he's back up in the hotel room with the camera and the crew.

Oh, she said, and looked around. I thought it just followed us wherever we went.

Would that it could have. She was magnificent, a Caribbean/ Irish Liverpudlian playing a difficult role, a woman defined by race and colour, in a world managed by men. It was a strange confluence of issues the story brought to light: race, sexuality, class, everything turned on its head by a set of misunderstandings. Bob was that emotional Russian doll: you would unscrew one lid only to find another layer of emotion underneath.

If *The Company of Wolves* had some success, *Mona Lisa* had more, won Bob Hoskins the Palme d'Or at Cannes, was nominated for Golden Globes and one Oscar, again for Bob. I had heard audiences laugh for the first time at one of my films.

The scenes between Robbie Coltrane and Bob were a welcome relief from the intensity of the overall drama. Something about laughter maybe makes you think you've got it right, but that is no reason for the presumption that you can make a comedy. Anyway, I found it so gratifying that I sketched out a little story that I had read in a newspaper, about a tour bus operator who was guiding tourists around apparently haunted houses. I remembered Oscar Wilde's 'The Canterville Ghost'. I remembered a short John Ford had made, called *A Minute's Wait*. I remembered the Alexander Mackendrick comedies, *The Man in the White Suit* and *Whisky Galore!* I developed a comedy of manners about a set of relationships between the living and the dead. I thought it could be made in black and white, in a small production, in the West of Ireland.

My producers at Palace were anxious to 'crack the American market'. They had tried and failed with the extravagant *Absolute Beginners*. They had succeeded with the under-the-radar *Mona Lisa*. They read my humble outline and thought this would be their real opportunity.

High Spirits

The baby-faced executive
has only so much time to give
The VPs file in through the door
your current script is on the floor
a tasteful parquet, newly done
to signify the Brits have come
they ask why it's not like your last
you tell them that emotion's past
they say your forte seems to be
film noir and not filmed comedy
I thought I'd try my hand at farce
you mumble, thinking what these ass-
holes need to hear is repartee
so try a line or two to see
how it goes down and when it dies
you hit them with some other ploys
it's visual so that all the laughs
come out of what you'll photograph
the bed that falls down through the floor
that's not been seen on screen before

the bus that rises from the bog
means more than all the dialogue
a deft amalgam of what's best
in Quiet Man *and* Ghost Goes West
the classic form, the current theme
the surreal logic of a dream
then seeing their attention wane
you try another tack again
the gore, the blood, the sex, the crack
the fun is necrophiliac
they smile politely, not too much
promise that they'll be in touch
we'd love to work with you someday
if not on this we'll find a way
I like your suit, what's your hotel?
you hear the elevator bell
you swing your budget rent-a-car
left on Santa Monica
you crash a light, then hit a kerb
and scream a solitary verb
the bimbo in the left-hand lane
screams it back at you again
your driving's bad,
your script's a mess
your credit card is creditless
you're melting slowly in the haze
that typifies Los Angeles
you threaten to, if things get worse,
go back to writing awful verse
you only ever said you'd come

so postcards might impress your mum
so buy one while the going's good
your loving son in Hollywood.

Neil Jordan and Daryl Hannah.

Hollywood

I do remember a moment, walking across the lot at Columbia with one of those American partners, a producer who seemed to have stepped straight from Mel Brooks's *The Producers*, when I knew I should call it off. I phoned Anton Furst, who had begun building the sets at Shepperton Studios. You can't, he told me. This is my best work.

Your best work, I thought. OK, I had better continue.

So, now it's maybe time to say something about the state of mind that is Los Angeles.

I loved the place, and could never work out why. The drive from the Hollywood Hills down to Santa Monica and Sunset, the light on Mulholland Drive, the spectacle of the valley to one side, West Hollywood and Century City and the infinite Pacific on the other. The Pacific Coast Highway, out to Point Dume and beyond, the drive to Santa Barbara. I made the oddest friends there, and again couldn't explain why. Warren Beatty, Frank Zappa, Carrie Fisher, Nick Nolte.

I also hated the place, and knew exactly why.

David Puttnam had just taken over at Columbia Pictures, promising to cleanse Hollywood excesses with a stern dose of British Realism. He hated Beatty, claimed his picture *Reds* was emblematic of all the worst excesses of Hollywood and gave Beatty reason to hate him. The fact that Puttnam had, probably wisely, rejected my script, might have given Warren reason to befriend me, but I'm not sure. Hollywood was always more complicated than that. These masters of their own universe were perched on this desert on the edge of their own continent, with nothing but the vast Pacific between themselves and Asia. They ruled a kingdom that seemed to be in a constant state of decay. The question always being, what must it have been like, when? In the seventies, sixties, fifties, forties? There was a golden age that had been tarnished irretrievably, but that was always on the point of reinvention. Who or what was to blame for the current state of things? Spielberg and George Lucas, that's who, *Jaws* and *Star Wars*, that's what. There was a time when a movie could sit for months in the same theatre, find its audience and then move on. The Blockbuster destroyed that. Don Simpson and Jerry Bruckheimer, that's who. The High Concept destroyed the Blockbuster. Bruce Willis has just stepped from television into an enormous paycheck. What does that make me worth? TV ruined everything in the fifties. DVD gets in the ruination act, then streaming. Everything is ruined anyway, that was the feeling. The whole place is in a perpetual state of decay, from a perfection that probably never existed. That Woody Allen film, *Midnight in Paris*, where Owen Wilson takes a mysterious taxi back to past decades; in each of them there are characters who lament the current state of cultural decay and wish they were working in the previous decade could have been set in Los Angeles. Maybe it was about Los Angeles.

And yet. The sense of waste when the rains came down. The towers of downtown against a grey, cloudy sky. This was a dangerous place. The *Los Angeles Times*, some mornings, perused over breakfast in Hamburger Hamlet, seemed as much a catalogue of murders as it did of Hollywood deals. Despite all the violence downtown, everyone in the Hollywood Hills left their doors open. Those sweet bungalows in Laurel and Benedict Canyon had always got a strange smell, which seemed to come from the basements below. The smell of mulch and decay. I could write a book about this place, I thought. What I shouldn't do is make a film about this place.

Warren Beatty called me early one morning and said 'He's gone'.

'Who's gone?' I asked, wondering why I'd be privy to any such information.

'Puttnam. Be announced later today.'

And indeed it was announced, later that day.

This was a brutal place.

Anton Furst had a development deal with Universal Pictures. They wanted him to come with a film for Michael Jackson.

And indeed you could imagine Michael Jackson in one of Anton's creations, the same flying Batmobile for which he'd just won an Oscar. He was also designing Planet Hollywood. He was in demand and utterly exhausted.

He checked himself into Cedars-Sinai Medical Center with the help of Nigel Phelps, his assistant.

While Nigel was signing the papers, he went searching for a place he could smoke. It was always a pipe, with Anton.

He took the elevator to the roof of the building and jumped onto Beverly Boulevard, below.

It was a brutal place.

How It Was

I have a dream. I'm at a party, or reception, I'm not sure which. It has something to do with advertising. A group of salesmen enter who have developed new techniques to sell coffins. They are expert palmists. One look at your hand tells them when you will need it and how long you have to make your advance payments. They read my palm. Three weeks, they mutter. Pay us in cash.

I'm staying in the only bungalow available in the motel where John Belushi killed himself. The suspicion that it might be *the* one occurs to me every morning at roughly the same time, 4.30, when I sit bolt upright, wide awake with the uneasy impression that a stoned spirit has passed from the bedroom to the fridge. My imagination, which can work wonders, generally lies, so I attempt to get back to sleep. If it was a spirit it was definitely stoned, I tell myself, in a woozy opiate haze with no bad intentions. But sleep doesn't come and the pale orange light is beginning its march beyond the blinds. I know this light and habits very well. It begins orange and lightens to a sliver on the wall opposite me. This sliver grows imperceptibly into an elegant rectangle, long, stretching from ceiling to floor. Now, although it grows, I can never see it move. A minor miracle in itself, I tell myself.

And as it grows, the colour of the light changes. From that orange, to amber, to the hue of dusty chalk. And as it changes, the rectangle widens, creates two minor, angled extensions on the ceiling and floor. And all these processes happen at once. And never, never can I observe the act of changing, can only monitor the result.

Such are the delights of insomnia. And when recalled in retrospect, in the peace of one's home where the habit of drinking is not so despised and thus sleep is more readily available, they do seem like delights. But at the time, ten minutes' oblivion would more than compensate for all such observation. And sleep won't come, so observe it I must. And only when the light turns truly banal – when it's flooded the whole wall and assumed the colour of pale vomit – do I get up, put on my clothes and drive.

I drive because I need company, any kind of company, instead of the isolation that seems the norm here. My car, parked in the wrong place, has a ticket glued to the windscreen. I can never get the hang of those things. I drive because the company of these strange, intent beings on their way to work is preferable to the company of nothing. I turn left down to Sunset and then make a right.

The street hoardings advertise the coming movies. Once I longed to get my name on one of those hoardings. I felt that people whose names were on those hoardings didn't end up doing things like watching the light come up when they couldn't sleep; they felt warmer than that, they belonged – they had their names on hoardings after all. Then when my

name did come to be on a hoarding, a little one, tucked away
to the side so that only very inattentive drivers would get to see
it, I thought: this is not the feeling I'd expected, not the feeling
I'd waited all those years for, with bated breath, the way the
shyest daughter waits for her wedding night. No, this is not
the thing at all. I didn't feel more warm, more secure, I didn't
belong to anything, I only felt stupid, standing with Stephen
Woolley in the middle of both lanes, cars hooting, saying get
the fuck out, and somehow I knew then that having your name
on hoardings was no guarantee whatsoever of untroubled
sleep. In fact it made you sleep worse because you thought,
why didn't they get a better hoarding, why do they have to be
such cheapskates, maybe if the name was bigger or had a little
line underneath it the way some names do, maybe that's the
thing. And so you're awake once more, and you know that's
not the thing, that's not the thing at all.

And for all this I wept not, I who wept for Dido slain.

So anyway, I'm driving, a pathetic substitute for company.
I'm looking for a restaurant serving breakfast at this hour. I
know if I stop at one that is not quite yet open, that opens in
ten minutes, a muddle will occur, one of those muddles that
gives you the equivalent waking feeling of sitting bolt upright
from your sleep. Something has made you uneasy and you
don't know what it is. You suspect it is you, of course, everyone suspects it is you, deep down in your heart you know it is
you, and this mild confusion has only served to confirm your
worthlessness. No, restaurants that are not yet open, or only
half open, are to be avoided.

I find one, though – one that is open – and with the ease, the
sense of belonging of a true man of the world, I slide beneath

the sign that says Restaurant Parking. Now, approaching my view, is the gentleman whose job it is to open your car door, hand you a ticket, smile politely and park it. Now, someone who had driven in search of company, it would be assumed, would exchange some words, no matter how inconsequential with such a person. But for some reason I don't. I merely smile politely, thank him and walk towards the door. Now there's a strange thing. And walking in I ask myself why. Because it is not the done thing. I tell myself.

Now the restaurant is there, I enter the low door, it goes dark for a while and then the inside makes itself known to me. There is a smiling girl behind a cash desk and behind her a kind of conservatory with seats for diners. Waiters, with a somehow European sense of boredom, are lounging on the seats.

Now, I know I need a paper to have breakfast with. A newspaper helps, in an indefinable way, somehow someone sitting with a newspaper knows what he's about; he has things to do, he's not just sitting having breakfast because he can't sleep. No, he eats as he peruses, he belongs. So I ask the girl for change for a dollar bill. In her slightly puzzled face I can see the first hint of a major muddle; the first cloud forms, a slight shiver of terror like the one caused by the stoned ghost who walked to the fridge. The first thing you do when you walk into a restaurant is ask for change. Explain yourself, something whispers, so I do. It's for a newspaper, I say, and grin, awkwardly, pointing to the row of newspaper receptacles on the pavement outside. She smiles as if she understands and the muddle passes. Thank you, I tell her, with inordinate gratitude. I make my way out again, through the other door, to the white sunlight out there and the pavement.

A word about these newspaper receptacles. First, about the nomenclature. The name I've chosen is the wrong one: they don't receive newspapers, they dispense them, after you've deposited a quarter in the tiny slot. They are simple, squat, metallic things with a glass panel to display the particular brand of newspaper imprisoned beneath. And I know brand is the wrong word, too, it seems to turn newspapers into soap powder, but I am in a foreign country, trying to understand. Now the newspaper receptacles, which they don't have in London or Dublin, seem simple, ingenious solutions to the problem of dispensing newspapers without involving people. But there are hidden dangers. And the chief of them is this. Once having got your quarter from the waitress, who thankfully understands, the idea is that you drop the quarter in the slot, lift up the glass panel and take out the newspaper of your choice, which you are now free to read. But if, in your haste, or your misunderstanding of the process, or through a pathetic attempt to be different about things, you attempt to pull the glass panel while your quarter is still rattling down the chute towards whatever home it finds in there, the glass panel will get stuck, the quarter will be lost, with – God forbid – no more quarters. A muddle, if ever there was one. You then have two options – if you have another quarter that is. You can retreat gracefully, and have your breakfast without the benefit of that form of discourse we call journalism, or you can try again. And if you try again, the following steps are recommended. First, shake the panel firmly to make sure it is unstuck. Then, taking another quarter out, slide it down the hole, and after what any instruction manual would define as a decent pause, attempt to raise the glass panel.

So the paper comes out, bound by a piece of a white plastic, a bundle of sections about one inch thick, to be placed under one's free arm as one resumes an attempt at breakfast. So I make my way back from the hot pavement to the brown interior where I catch the eye of the girl behind the cash machine, who gestures me towards an immaculate waiter, again with a decidedly European air, who leads me to a place by the window.

By now the streets are buzzing outside, the hum of the traffic is a pleasing drone, the morning sun cuts the room in half and a girl in a pink tracksuit enters through it. The waiter sits her at a table near the door and comes to take my order. I refuse his offer of coffee and ask for tea. Coffee here is a generic concept, but tea is a rarity: there are varieties of the stuff one doesn't find at home. English Breakfast, I explain, and he nods benignly and leaves. The thought of insomnia has abated now; it seems OK to be awake with someone else in the room. Her pink tracksuit is quite immaculate, the colour Irish mothers favour for newborn babies. She has been given a plate of cereal and is reading a book. She is remarkable in that she has perfectly even teeth. A couple enter, also remarkable for their perfect teeth. The waiter brings my tea, and smiles, exposing his perfect teeth. I am in a culture, I realize, that has brought the science of dentistry to heights undreamed of in my philosophy. In early adolescence the teeth are ringed by metal braces, creating a mouthful of gleaming silver so that in early adulthood one can smile with comfort. If the chin is receding, or its opposite, creating what is known as an overbite, the jaw can be surgically broken. For those of us with unbroken jaws, without the benefit of a steel-ringed adolescence, there is the option of keeping one's mouth shut.

Sipping tea without exposing one's rotting molars is not too difficult. Reading the pages of the *Los Angeles Times* is. A society where every fact is of equal interest, is reported with equal space and sonority, is one to be approached with circumspection. And such a society is Los Angeles, to judge from the pages of the *Los Angeles Times*. The acres of newsprint are endless, divided into alphabetical sections, devoted to world affairs, entertainment, civic affairs, fashion, cookery, property. And the dangers of muddle presented by the format are legion. I sit in my appointed place, balance the thing on my knee, try to break the piece of white plastic that binds it, and end up using the table knife.

It is the murders that interest me most, these triumphant expressions of contact in an isolated world. Currently running are the Millionaire Club Murders, the Cotton Club Murder, various serial treatments on serial killers and the ongoing saga of the gang killings. These are by far the most dramatic, with their portraits of young neighbourhood warriors with assault rifles, hand grenades, Uzis and rocket launchers. I read of how casualty wings have turned into battlefield hospitals. How medical techniques perfected in Beirut and Belfast are at a premium here. I remember a relative of a friend of mine who perfected a device known as the Sheehan knee, an artificial kneecap in great demand around Ballymurphy, and wonder whether I should give him a call. I wonder whether murder here has the same intimacy as it has at home and conclude that it must. The final, desperate expression of the need to have a chat.

But the day is in its element now and those peculiar traumas have passed. The restaurant is full, the place is buzzing and that peculiar self-loathing that happens in the twilight hours has gone. There are meetings to attend, calls to be made, the possibility of speech. I pay the waiter, smile without fear, grab the acres of newsprint into an awkward bundle and make my way outside, a citizen of something, of what I can't be sure, but then most others can't either.

Night comes and the muddle descends. I have to go to a preview of a movie I've made. The studio is nervous, the producers are nervous, the stream of traffic down Sunset seems to shake, I drive a convertible car with the hood down. The hood is down because I don't know how to get it up. The car, it seems, has some cachet since people wave at traffic lights, drivers of similar vehicles raise their heads in gestures of fellowship. I take the San Diego Freeway towards Long Beach and wonder at all the cars in the world. The signs flash by me with their unpronounceable, poetic names signalling the prosaic suburbs beneath. Taking the name of my destination at face value, I anticipate a mass of white strand, a boardwalk, a long beach. But that is always a mistake. The presumption that place names hold a clue to what they signify is a peasant's one. The punishment for such presumption is murder.

I take the exit that seems the right one and find myself in that concrete, indeterminate purgatory that goes on forever. Having forsaken all hope of a beach, I drive through the low-lit streets, past the gangs of kids at every corner, think to stop at a gas station to ask the way. A phalanx of body builders try to shake me down, and I think twice about it. I drive on. I can picture the worst form of insomnia now, the one where you drive and you can't sleep because you can't stop. Now that the broader picture of Long Beach has failed, I concentrate on the specific, Lakeland, Long Beach. Getting wise to these things, I suspect there'll be neither land nor lakes. A Mexican kid on a street corner tells me in his broken Spanish to go to Willow and turn right. I go to Willow and turn right and drive for an age and find Lakeland. It is a mall, a small village devoted to commerce. People gather there, work there, sell things there, but don't live there. And in the centre of this mall is a movie complex which is previewing my film. It is here, I suspect, that this isolation might end. I can see the cars and limos pulling up near the entrance and the queue of the chosen gathering at the desk.

A preview is a method of assessment. Movies are assessed in two ways: their playability and their want-to-see. The die for their want-to-sees is cast at the outset, with the script chosen, the director, but most importantly, the stars. But their playability hangs in the balance until they are shown. As with most aspects of film-making, the legends surrounding previews are numerous. About the movie previewed without its score, where the music got the highest ratings. About the movie previewed without its last reel. About the ones that scored high and bombed. But the reverse, I have been told, is never true.

And the thing about previews is that while the executives, agents and producers will tell you they mean nothing, you must never believe them. You must enter that theatre secure in the knowledge that they mean everything. So you must enter the theatre in a calm manner, never fumbling with the glass doors or pulling them the wrong way. Resist all urges to smoke a cigarette. Dress neither up nor down. Shake hands politely with those who have given you the equivalent of the gross national product of Uruguay to make this tender little piece. They will tell you they love it – and it will be true. Their affection for your film is as genuine as their support for you was during the making of it. But you can see the nervousness, the terror that it might not work, the awful suspicion that what was so lovingly nurtured and constructed might turn out to be art and nothing else. And that thing that is so longed for, that necessary frisson between class and commerce, will have retreated once more until the next time, if there is a next time.

So the house lights go down and the picture comes up. A comedy of sorts, made by you who can never tell a joke, who always blows the punchline. Shot in sombre colours, with an opening reel so dark as to be terrifying. And you begin to question every instinct you ever had, every choice you ever made, the very fact of your being born. Until the front titles end and the first shots come up. And a small ripple of laughter runs through the theatre. You are amazed; you never thought this was a laugh-out-loud comedy, more of a whimsical parable about escaped convicts, sin and redemption. But the ripples of laughter continue. No one walks out.

Then there is the postmortem. The cards filled out. Did they grade the film excellent, very good, good or poor. It gets so many points in the first two boxes. The thing, the bearded producer tells you, an unlit cigar between his teeth is to move the ratings from the good to the very good, and so on. Change ripples of laughter to gales of laughter. Bob De Niro's always best when he's broad. He was broad, he was moderate, he was understated. He seemed to enjoy giving a range of responses which you enjoyed, too. So this moderate, rather sweet, whimsical version will stay in the Columbia vaults. Lost, probably, like your hire car, in the vast parking lot. You've forgotten what level you parked it on. And each level now is a badly lit, crepuscular forest of shadows. Maybe you'll never find it again.

Movies I Haven't Made 2

*K*ing Lear, starring Marlon Brando.
 There was a message for me on the answering machine in the dusty room of the Chateau Marmont hotel. The Chateau's pretension then was that it wasn't a hotel at all, some kind of strange underground rooming service. The gent at the front desk had a uniform response when he lifted the phone. Chateau, not a question or even a statement, just a monotone that left all obligation to respond up to whoever was calling. A lift that took you from the parking lot into a large fake French chateau-like interior, and whatever thin, elegant gent was managing the front desk would barely look up when he (always a he then) took your room key from the rack behind him.

There was a message on my answering machine when I eventually made it to my room – with a huge billboard featuring the Marlboro Man and Sunset Boulevard outside. If you were special and needed discretion you probably got or were given, by whomever was paying the bill, a bungalow. I was neither special nor did I need discretion, but needed company, so when I saw the red light flashing on the phone by the bedside

I thought, with embarrassing delight, somebody actually called me! I lifted the phone and listened to the message and couldn't make head nor tail of it. A mumble. Who did I know that mumbled thus? I had no idea. Did I have something to do that evening? I don't remember. But the next morning, another flashing light, another message. This time the caller had left a number and I could work out the mumbled name. Marlon.

Could that actually be Marlon Brando? Then I remembered, I had been asked by my agent, Jeff Berg, what random ideas I had. I had spoken about how Brando seemed a Lear-like figure lately. His son had been in some horrible altercation with his sister's lover, which resulted in a death. The warring children, the king without a kingdom, and I had wondered would he ever consider playing Lear? But could Brando have actually called me? Left a message? I played the tape again, heard the mumbled message and made out the mumbled number and called it. You had to do that then. You actually had to scribble the number down on the hotel notepad and push in the relevant digits. And then the legendary voice came on the phone. It was indeed Marlon. And he would love to meet. When? I asked him. Anytime this morning.

How extraordinary, I thought. He must be lonely. Almost as lonely as me. So I drove, up Woodrow Wilson, through the winding canyons to Mulholland Drive, took the turn he had mentioned, entered a set of gates, through gardens with a Filipino gardener doing the lawns, to the forecourt. What do they call it? The turnaround. A much more descriptive and peremptory term. I loved the *reductio ad absurdum* of American usage. Particularly road signs. STOP. GO ON SLOW. WALK. DON'T WALK.

And this was a turnaround, not a forecourt. A dusty, gravelly circle surrounding some dusty shrubs. I parked the car, got out and approached the doorbell, expecting the usual palaver. A voice on the intercom saying Mr Brando's residence? But no. I had barely pressed the bell when the door opened and there he was. Dressed in a huge flowing kaftan, displaying a distressingly large belly, but the gaze and the bald head could have stepped straight out of the Cambodian jungle and *Apocalypse Now*.

You're Irish, he said.

I told him I was. He led me inside, into the empty house, into a kitchen, where he got us a juice, or some tea. There was a small patio outside, with some dusty orange trees. He took me out there, and plucked a small orange from one of the bushes, peeled it and offered me some.

I was in Ireland, a few years ago.

And I remembered. There was some benighted project that fell apart, with Johnny Depp, among others.

I came off the plane there, and driving out of the airport, when I went under that bridge – do you know that bridge?

He couldn't be talking about the same bridge, could he? The bridge over the Nanny, carrying the Drogheda to Dublin train.

From the airport into the city?

Yeah. The dark bridge.

I knew the bridge. It was the bridge on Drumcondra Road. Near the Cat and Cage. Or was it Fagan's? Near St Pat's, where my father taught for years.

Well, when I passed under that bridge, it was the first time I ever felt at home.

But wasn't he Italian? With some Native American? I didn't

want to ask. Then I remembered his strange accent in *The Missouri Breaks*. As if someone from a Christopher Marlowe play had wandered into Dion Boucicault's *The Shaughraun*.

So you're Irish?

Must be, he mumbled. He tore one of the oranges apart and began to suck the juice. I half expected him to put the orange peel over his teeth, the way he did before he keeled over in *The Godfather*.

Anyway, when I passed under that bridge, I felt at home, for the first time. In my life.

There was something sad about the way he said it. Something sad all around.

It's important, home. The feeling of home.

So you weren't at home as Terry Malloy, in *On the Waterfront*? I thought this, but didn't say it. Then I remembered the character was an Irish American stevedore.

I thought of him searching for a home in Tahiti in *Mutiny on the Bounty*. I had watched it with my mother in the Fairview Cinema. Did the dancing girls with their bare breasts covered with garlands of flowers embarrass her? They certainly embarrassed me. Gave me an erection that was hard to hide.

A woman came to join us, who he introduced as his house-keeper. I had the feeling she was more than that, but she poured some tea. When she left us to it, he began describing the difficulties she experienced around Los Angeles, being Mexican. In shops and supermarkets. It seemed to upset him deeply, and he felt he should help her with the shopping, but he couldn't venture downtown himself.

We began talking projects then and I asked him had he ever thought of playing King Lear? He looked at me with those slow-lidded eyes and said no American actor can play Shakespeare.

But you did, I said, in – and I had to click my fingers, trying to remember the name. *Julius Caesar.*

I didn't play Julius Caesar. I played Mark Antony.

Mark Antony. Of course. In the film of *Julius Caesar*—

You see, you couldn't remember. Which allows me to rest my case. No American actor can play Shakespeare.

And not being entirely approving of the Royal Shakespeare traditions of acting, I had to disagree.

No English actor can play Shakespeare either.

Aha, I thought. Now we're getting to the nub of things.

And then he proceeded to a series of extraordinary note-perfect imitations of every English actor who ever had. Laurence Olivier. John Gielgud. Even Paul Scofield, in Peter Brook's filmed version of *King Lear*.

Maybe you're afraid, I ventured, of learning all those lines.

No, he said. I would have an earpiece for that.

And why do you use an earpiece?

Because none of us know what we're going to say next. Do you know what you're going to say next?

I did, actually, but he had a point.

So if I did play Shakespeare, ever again, I would do it as if I never knew what the next word was going to be.

An extraordinary and devastatingly simple reduction of the whole idea of acting, I had to admit.

But he was tired of acting. Didn't want to act again, let alone King Lear. What he wanted to do was perform magic tricks.

Look, he said, and pulled a small silk handkerchief from beneath his closed thumb.

You're wearing a false thumb, Marlon, I wanted to say. But I couldn't bring myself to.

Want to see how I did it?

Absolutely.

And he exposed what was indeed a false, plastic thumb.

I want you to have this.

I'll take it back to Ireland. I'll say hello to that bridge for you. I'll give it to my daughter.

But my daughter wasn't that impressed, when I finally made it home. You have better magic tricks yourself, she said. The one where you made the penny disappear, pressed into the palm of the innocent accomplice. And he was too much Lear to play him.

Tricks

I had a need of magic tricks, though. From being in a state where everything worked, I was in a state where nothing really worked. I had published a novel, in between several films that didn't work. My publisher, Carmen Callil, said you have to stop, do nothing but write, fiction as a continuum, not as an eruption every now and then between movies. But the problem was, I loved writing them, too.

I had sketched out a story after I wrote *Angel* that I called 'The Soldier's Wife'. A republican activist kidnaps a black British soldier and is the inadvertent cause of his death. I suppose 'inadvertent' is a bit of a cop-out. Any kidnapping implies and brings with it the threat of death. But what fascinated me, around that bloody time, and all of the talk of the pathology of terrorism, was that the problem wasn't pathology. The problem with the Provisional IRA wasn't that they were pathological. The problem was terrifyingly, spookily rational. They had political aims and made the appalling decision to pursue them pathologically.

That was one thing. The other was that the appearance of black British soldiers on the streets of Northern Ireland was for many Irish people their first encounter with issues of race. Brendan Behan had an interesting observation on his first visit to London (before, I imagine, he was arrested for his inept involvement in an earlier bombing campaign). He saw a West Indian navvy on a building site, shovelling earth from a deep hole with other navvies from the West of Ireland. He was astounded. His only encounter with non-white races up to then had been impeccably dressed Nigerian student doctors entering and exiting the College of Surgeons on St Stephen's Green.

Now, the appearance of West Indian squaddies on the streets of Belfast led to appalling outpourings of racism from the oppressed minority they were sent there to defend. Or eventually patrol, and oppress, depending on your point of view. So there were multiple ironies here, and I had sketched out a story that could maybe explore them.

There was a precedent, of course, for such a story, given that there is nothing original under the sun: a short story by Frank O'Connor, called 'Guests of the Nation', that examined the kidnapping of a British squaddie in an earlier conflict. An Irish-language play by Brendan Behan about another story of a kidnapped soldier, called *An Ghiall*, which was turned into a major West End success by Joan Littlewood as *The Hostage*.

In my version of it, which took both versions as just a starting point, the kidnapper has to flee to London, adopt a new identity and under the cover of that identity befriends the dead soldier's wife. Hence the title.

But every time I moved the story to London (after what a Hollywood screenwriter would call the first act) I came to a juddering halt. What had been full of drama, intensity and danger became kitchen-sink. And while basic realism was a huge strength of British cinema, it held no interest for me. Or maybe I was just no good at it. Dreams, fantasies, the stuff underneath the real were what I always needed to drive things forward.

I had a strange thought then and it was so insane it needed examining. What if the wife of the title was not actually a woman but a man. What if the picture the squaddie shows his captor, of a beautiful mixed-race woman, turned out to be a man in disguise? A transvestite, a transexual, someone we would now call of trans identity. There was already enough of a subdued sexual dynamic in the scenes of captivity. Any captor has to play mother to his captive, has to feed him, lead him to the toilet, even unzip him and take his thing out. Unless he unchains his hands, which he can't. Chain him, unchain him and the metaphor of bondage in that situation can go two ways. If Fergus (the suitably nationalistic name I gave to the captor) can be played by Jody (the name I gave to the squaddie) in a teasing, flirtatious, sexual manner, and enjoys the sense of titillation he can get from the beautiful picture of his wife, the basic game of captivity could extend itself through the rest of the scenario. The story could then be designed to assault every facet of what Fergus presumes is his identity. He is Irish, he is white, he is male. He will be forced to confront a reality that is British, that is black, that is neither male nor female. It was an immediately more interesting prospect. And it filled the London scenes with an undertow, a sense of immanence and discovery.

And maybe that's always been my problem with London. It is too realistic a city. I would shoot in it three times, *Mona Lisa*, *The Crying Game*, *The End of the Affair*, and each time have had to work hard, maybe even too hard, to turn it into an existential playground. The happy domesticity of *Notting Hill* and *Paddington* was not for me. *Alice in Wonderland*, maybe, or yet another version of *Great Expectations*. The murderous river of *Our Mutual Friend*. *Dracula*, without a doubt.

I had a solution. To my issues with London, with 'Guests of the Nation', with yet another iteration of that dreary scenario, the terrorist on the run. I sent it – to whom? Stephen Woolley, I suppose, because no one else would be foolhardy enough to take on such a project. And to Stephen Rea, since if there was anyone who could bring this character to life it had to be him.

So you've got a screenplay that deals with the issues of race, terror and what will soon be called gender identity. Who will finance it? Nobody, that's who. Every studio turns it down, every sales agent. Harvey Weinstein, who runs Miramax and is the great god of independent cinema, says he will consider it if I cast a woman as the transexual.

Now why would that be, Harvey?

Because, he reasons, the audience will be so disgusted if they find out it is a man.

I did a series of tests, to see if the illusion could even be established and maintained. On Harvey's advice, did Cathy Tyson the great indignity of testing her, along with several males. What became immediately obvious was that only if a man played the role would it make any sense.

We got backing from Channel Four eventually, on one condition. That I rewrite the ending. Which I dutifully did. I wrote an ending that referenced the film beloved of all transgressives – *Some Like It Hot*. I even, and I'm not sure I'm remembering this correctly, referenced the line 'nobody's perfect'. This thing I'd written, apparently, would only become acceptable if it came coated in sugar.

But we had now, apparently, a budget and a start date. But no actor to play the love interest, whom I had called, for some reason not even clear to myself, Dil.

I paid another visit out to St Albans and had another Chinese dinner with Stanley Kubrick. Had he read the script? I don't remember. Maybe I had told him the story. He said, you're looking for a black actor to play a woman and you're shooting when?

In about a month, I told him.

Make that two years, he said.

It was a different way of operating, I was aware. He wouldn't have allowed such an imponderable to enter into any equation. But I was shooting in a month. And I had just met Jaye Davidson.

Derek Jarman had told Sandy Powell about a beautiful creature he had met on the demi-monde of the club scene. Jaye was an extraordinary, almost self-created being. He had never thought of acting, had worked in fashion, and, actually, if I can believe the legend, worked on the team that created Lady Diana's wedding dress. Anyway, he was as skittish as a young colt, and as flickery as, to continue the Diana theme, a candle in the wind. But he could without a doubt create the illusion. He could be a woman who turned out to be a man.

But could he act? It was almost beside the point. Non-actors have an edgy, dangerous quality to them. They keep practised actors on their toes. Everything they do is done for the first time and can rarely be repeated. Using someone who's never acted before, had no thought of acting or of the procedural niceties of it can be like introducing a wild animal into a petting farm. So, yes, it seemed appropriate, given the subject matter, which seemed to make the whole world of movie production afraid. And, besides, we had no alternative. Nobody else could, literally, fit the clothes.

Jaye was a gay man, a beautiful and at the time a very feminine gay man. But as he said to me, he hadn't a trans bone in his body. He was very stridently himself and didn't share the vulnerability of the character I had written. I had to populate the environment around him with trans characters, most particularly the bar which I had called the Metro. And so I got to meet this extraordinary community. It was the very early days of what is now called transitioning, many of them were men who dressed and lived as women, and would have termed themselves transvestites, but others were going through the early and late stages of hormone treatment before a medical procedure and others had finished the procedure themselves. Male to female, given the theme of the film, and the bar. And what I found extraordinary is that many of them in the early stages of transition were Irish and had an experience that paralleled the story of the film. Had met a man, as a woman, and felt no need to declare their issues at the start. As the relationship progressed, the point came where physical contact was inevitable and the response from their prospective partner would be a shrug, or an embrace, or the line, I already knew, darling...

Fergus couldn't know, and there would lie a problem.

Jaye was dressed by Sandy Powell for his first scene, which would be crossing a cricket pitch and ascending scaffolding to the building site in which Stephen Rea was wielding a sledgehammer, working on demolition. I had prepared that scene quite carefully, because I remember the situation from many years ago. Not the memory of being met by a beautiful, feminine boy on a building site, but the experience of slamming down a wall with a sledgehammer and exposing, through the crumbling, dusty brick, a scene of idyllic, pastoral England. A cricket pitch which gradually revealed itself through the falling haze. Figures in white, bowling on a green expanse and the distant crack of bat against ball.

Sandy had dressed Jaye in cut-off jeans, a pair of stacked heels and a leather top. Clothes Marc Bolan could have worn or any recent disciple of the New Romantics. He could have been a girl or a boy or a time traveller from the eighteenth century crossing that pitch. But he could have only been one character, ascending that scaffolding lift. Dil, terrified of rejection, but determined to confront the Fergus who had misunderstood her. Jaye was as nervous as she would have been, voice breaking under the strain of really acting for the first, real time. Beads of sweat appearing on his upper lip. It was as fragile as a piece of bone china, but it was undeniably real. And beautiful.

It is odd, that feeling that you have a story on your hands. And not only a story, a character. I had chosen Dave Berry's song 'The Crying Game' for Dil to sing in the Metro bar. I remembered it from when I was a kid, listening to the rain hit the corrugated roof of the dancehall in Laytown. Dave Berry had made strange gestures on his *Top of the Pops* appearances, tracing imaginary moonbeams falling from above with his fingers. Jaye did the same, appearing from behind a Chinese screen in a gold lamé dress. The effect was mesmerizing, and somehow, pop.

The Crying Game. *Jaye Davidson*
and Miranda Richardson.

So we followed the character and the character followed the story, and Stephen Rea falls in love with a woman he knows he shouldn't have even approached. Not because of any gender issues, but because he has basically killed her husband. And the moment comes when physical intimacy becomes inescapable. We had dressed Dil's bedroom in reddish scarves thrown over bed lamps, which gave the set an eerie, pinkish light. Jaye comes in for the scene of the revelation of what he is, and underneath the black, silk Japanese kimono I had chosen, was wearing a pair of pink silk underpants. I had guided the character, been convinced by it, surprised by the performance at every turn. But this was a surprise I wasn't ready for.

I took his dresser aside. Asked him does Jaye not know he has to be naked in this scene? He looked shocked and shook his head.

I don't think Jaye would ever agree to that. Have never even discussed that with him.

I remembered my conversations with some of those transitioning. Maybe Jaye, like the character, had a secret? The secret being in his case that he had already gone through an operation.

I sometimes wonder what would have been the result if that was actually the case. Quite different, without a doubt, from the shot that ended up in the film. I looked back at Jaye, his slim, taut chest underneath the kimono. There was no hormone treatment evident there, but then again, one never knew.

I took him aside and said as gently as possible that he had to take the shorts off, beneath the kimono.

Oh, he said, genuinely surprised, you want me to be naked underneath? No problem.

And there was no problem as it turned out. The only problem was with the reaction of Fergus when he realizes. He dry-retches in the sink, and backhands his lover, Dil, when she responds, I thought you knew.

Would he have done so? I don't know. Some in the trans community have taken exception to it. But the point was, he genuinely didn't know. If he had not been shocked, there would have been no drama. If he had not been shocked, there could have been no genuine reconciliation.

We were approaching the end of the shoot and came to the awful moment where the fake ending was scheduled. An appalling travesty of what had gone before involving a remote-controlled Louma crane, a closed-off street, Christmas shoppers with wrapped parcels, fake snow and Stephen Rea returning to the scene of his first meeting with Jaye in Millie's hairdressers.

It was interesting how everything about it was immediately wrong. The fake snow, the expense of the camera crane, the overdressed crowd, the refurbished hairdressers. And wrongest of all was what the scene said, the debonair reappearance of Mr Rea, like Harry Lime in a sanitized, kitsch Vienna, unpunished for his actions, reconciled with his loved one as if it had been a Hollywood romantic comedy. I begged the producers not to shoot it, and to put the money elsewhere. I probably should have refused, but they would have closed the film down. So shoot it we did. Nobody's perfect.

But maybe I had to shoot it if only to make a public display of how terrible, how wrong it was. As the first rough cut showed. I was given the money to shoot a proper ending.

So we had a movie now, but nowhere to distribute it, nowhere to show it. We screened it for the Cannes Film Festival, who turned it down. Venice agreed to show it, but out of competition, as long as I agreed to serve on the jury. Stephen Woolley released it in the UK to a tepid and broadly contemptuous response. But then something began happening in North America.

It played the Toronto, Telluride and New York festivals to an ecstatic audience. Harvey Weinstein had to reconcile himself to the fact that an audience could respond emotionally to a man who seemed to be a woman. He bought the movie for the US and I had the foresight to ask my agent to insist on a clause that the picture cut could not be changed. I circulated a letter to critics begging them to find a way to discuss the movie without revealing the plot, and, to everyone's amazement, they all complied. If there was money to be made, Harvey and his brother Bob were the ones to make it. It was irritating, but probably inevitable that he would publicize it as 'the film with a secret'. And even when Jaye Davidson was nominated for an Oscar as best actor, that Weinstein would still push it as the film with a secret. Full-size posters of Jaye and Stephen on Hollywood Boulevard celebrating both the Oscar nominations and the secret.

But the problem, as always with the Weinsteins, was money. The film took a sizeable fortune in the US and worldwide, was made by a crew, myself included, that had deferred almost the totality of their fees on the understanding that they would be profit participants. Harvey and Bob had, before spending a penny on their US release, demanded waivers to those agreements from the cast and the crew. And even from Channel Four, the principal financiers.

But the film had taken more than seventy million dollars in the US, been nominated for six Oscars, won one, and taken the same again worldwide. I found it embarrassing, shameful. I even quoted the Bible: 'For the scripture saith, thou shalt not muzzle the ox when he treadeth the corn. And, the labourer is worthy of his hire.'

I had meetings with the producers, and with Channel Four. I demanded that they sue, to get a fair share of the profits for the cast and crew. They refused. Each of them, in their different ways, was tied to the Harvey ticket. As the lawyers for Channel Four told me, it was a black swan event, a one in a million windfall and they wanted to continue the relationship.

And why, I asked them, invest in independent movies if you can never participate in such a windfall?

Such was the allure of Miramax at the time, the almost mesmeric influence of Weinstein himself. They all wanted to work with him again.

I couldn't understand their reasoning, but had to swallow it. I won an Oscar for Best Screenplay, but didn't thank Weinstein. I don't think we ever had a meaningful conversation again.

And all this was before the sex crimes, the accusations of rape, the attempts to intimidate witnesses. I felt for him, I have to admit, when I saw him shuffle on a walker into that New York courtroom. I wondered which of those who'd submitted to him so cravenly would visit him in prison. But what I basically felt was he should have been tried for theft, long before.

Movies I Haven't Made 3

R *ed Harvest.*
     After I had made *Mona Lisa*, Alberto Grimaldi came to me with this book, by Dashiell Hammett. He had produced Fellini's *Satyricon*, Pasolini's *Salò*, Bertolucci's *Last Tango In Paris*, *1900*, and a string of spaghetti westerns. I can still see him, a small, besuited man walking to my house outside the promenade in Bray with his son, Roberto. He had long held the rights to the Hammett novel and commissioned a script by Bertolucci, but they had fallen out. Apparently *1900* lost all the money made by *Last Tango*. He asked me to write my own version, which I did, full of hard-boiled nuances and retribution.

The anti-hero, the Continental Op, travels in a train towards a mining town called Personville, which a New York layabout in the seat opposite pronounced as Poisonville.

The place is run by gangs, a corrupt police chief and even more corrupt mining magnates. He takes what would become a familiar route to clean it up. Sets them all against each other and enjoys the spectacle of them tearing their world apart.

I scouted locations with Anton Furst before his untimely death.

We flew up to Butte, Montana, where Hammett had worked as a Pinkerton detective and where he set the book. It was full of abandoned copper mines and signs from the Anaconda Copper Mining Company saying, 'Land Poisoned, Keep Out'. So the mispronunciation, Poisonville, turned out to be appropriate.

Oddly enough, most of the miners were Irish, from the copper mines of the Beara Peninsula, West Cork.

We flew in small planes to Timmins, Ontario and Yellowknife in the Northwest Territories, mining towns all over. We eventually settled on Albany, New York. They had shot *Ironweed* there, and I met its writer, William Kennedy, with an Irish poet, John Montague. John was a boxer as well as a poet, he told me, but he'd left his pugilistic talents at home. He was here giving a creative writing course, a fate, he told me, that awaits all Irish writers. He could see I was doing my best to avoid it.

There was a skeleton in the closet, though. The film had already been made – transplanted to medieval Japan by Kurosawa – *Yojimbo*. And I don't think anyone could have bettered that.

Sergio Leone disagreed. He remade *Yojimbo* in turn as *A Fistful of Dollars* and introduced Clint Eastwood to the world.

Maybe that's why Alberto couldn't interest a studio. He was about to lose the rights to the book, so he came up with a unique way of retaining them. He hired an Italian director to shoot the cheapest possible version of the entire film in Almería in Spain and destroyed the negative.

I can only imagine the feelings of that director, whoever he was. Shooting a film, knowing the negative of each day's work was going to be burned. Did they use my script? Did they use Bernardo's?

Maybe he exists in a parallel universe. His *Red Harvest* was released to great acclaim, after the extraordinary success of his *Lear*, with Marlon Brando. He then went on to work for Disney, on a musical space epic, with murderous rhyming teddy bears.

Suddenly

I seemed to fall in love the way Hemingway went bankrupt. Gradually, and then suddenly.

With the woman who came to work for me in the house in Bray it was very gradual, then very sudden. She wore a green dress, I remember – or maybe she remembers – and I was wearing a green tracksuit having come from a desultory run along the promenade. I had two daughters to look after, for a good half of every week, and a house full of printed materials. Scripts I had begun and not finished, drafts of novels, published and unpublished. Like most separated fathers, I was a bit of a mess, but it was a mess I enjoyed and they enjoyed, too. There was a freedom in living alone, in having your girls come for long weekends, having a regretful but fond relationship with your ex-wife, although that status wouldn't be regularized until divorce was finally allowed under the Irish Constitution, in the constitutional referendum of 1996. What I do remember is the extreme watchfulness of my two daughters over any woman who threatened to disturb this equilibrium. There had been several, and the results weren't good. But they seemed to like this Brenda, from Canada, who lived with a bearded

Brenda, Neil and Jaye.

Protestant gentleman in a house in Kilcroney, Co. Wicklow. She needed the work, I needed the assistance, so why would things change?

I can remember the exact moment they changed for me, although maybe she can't. She was showing me how a new printer worked, pressing various buttons, bending over it to feed in the paper. Was she wearing the green dress? I can't be sure. Though I can be certain that something happened, for me if not for her.

How can you fall in love over a printer? The most boring of office machines, the most irritating, for anyone who writes. Over a black Olivetti typewriter from the 1930s, maybe, even over an electric Remington from the 1960s, with one of those bobbing golf ball-like gizmos that hold all of the alphabet. I can imagine the sound, the clack clack clack, the cigarette smoke in the air, the sun coming through the office window over Sunset Boulevard or 13th Street or Île Saint-Louis or whatever garret this fantasy could be set in, the thrum like a woodpecker's beak of the golf ball alphabet. The wwwhttt as she pulls out the page. But over a printer in a disused front-room office looking out over the Irish Sea? Maybe there are gods in these affairs that know more than we do. Maybe the more mundane the setting, the more memorable, the more congruent their work.

Anyway, something happened and when something happens, even the best of us can be doomed. The suddenness for me was alarming; there had been a long gradually before that and an even longer gradually after, so maybe Hemingway's aphorism has to be turned on its head. Or twisted a bit. Gradually, then suddenly, then gradually again. There is a kind of exquisite dance that goes on, though, when you know something internal has happened that may never express itself. The bearded Protestant gentleman went first. There were a few other suitors, one from America, several from England, there were even confidences. Should I? Is this the one? No, dear assistant, that's not the one. He doesn't deserve you.

It took the First Gulf War, for some obscure reason, to consummate our relationship. This will not stand, the elder Bush said, and sure enough, it could not, would not, stand. The situation was beyond intolerable.

We saw the declaration of 'Shock and Awe' on a television in a chipper in Blackrock. We took our ray and chips back to her rented room behind, overlooking the Irish Sea. There's only one thing to do, when the world is ending. Let the Tomahawk missiles ejaculate from the USS *Theodore Roosevelt*, let Wolf Blitzer watch them sail past his Baghdad hotel room, let the oilfields blacken the desert sky. The grave's a fine and private place but none, I think, do there embrace. But maybe Dusty Springfield said it better than Andrew Marvell. It's crazy but it's true. I only want to be with you.

And the world didn't end after all.

Movies I Haven't Made 4

I do an awful lot of walking, Neil.

For some reason my children always called me by my first name. Maybe I had them too young. Ben did, although he didn't live with me. (There was no possibility of that.) I used to think that father, daddy, pater, dad, da were all learned affectations. If left to themselves they would call you what they wanted.

I was walking with Ben, up a hillside. He hated walking and I did an awful lot of it and so, by necessity, did he. I told him he was about to have a brother, to me and Brenda. Eventually he had had two.

Daniel and Dashiel, and they, thank goodness, lived with me. I sketched out a film that three boys might enjoy.

Hamlet.

Not Shakespeare's. The Hamlet of Saxo Grammaticus.

A very bad title, I know. Which could be improved. *The Danish Idiot?*

But every boy would love the Danish original of the story Shakespeare based his Hamlet on. And realize, if he was working for Blumhouse at the moment, he would have been so fired.

It's a beautifully elemental drama of revenge. Like an origin story for a superhero. The young Amleth's father is killed by his uncle, who assumes the kingship and marries his mother. Amleth's response to this trauma is to pretend to be an idiot – an early, drooling Danish version of PTSD. He sits by the enormous fireplace in the castle, unable to speak, making strange toys out of discarded bits of wood and metal. Everyone of course thinks he has lost his marbles. Until he comes to manhood, and we realize these strange toys make a series of weapons with which he kills the lot of them.

And of course becomes something like a manga warrior, the regicidal revenger...

No soliloquys. No gravedigger. No Rosencrantz and Guildenstern. I don't even think there is an Ophelia.

Bridges

Bridges. They must have meant something to me, from some old childhood memory. There was an old-fashioned bridge over the River Nanny, near my mother's birthplace in Mornington. What was unique about this bridge was that as the train from Drogheda thunders over, you would walk alongside the tracks, on a small parallel walkway. When I started making films, I shot Stephen Rea against this bridge, wandering in his electric-blue showband suit through the estuary below. For the opening of my second film, *The Company of Wolves*, I was at a reception at a festival in Los Angeles, shaking hands with Princess Anne, of all people, when I got news that my father had died, underneath that same bridge.

I was confused by Princess Anne. I found her sexually attractive and couldn't work out why. Was it the rather militaristic outfit she was wearing, the braids across the shoulders, like an admiral in some navy that sailed the seas for some Disney epic that hadn't yet been made? Was it the rather protruding teeth, the full lips that couldn't quite hide their prominence? Was it a secret gay thing that I had until then kept hidden? She looked like a personable male, with a peaked cap that wouldn't

Michael Collins – *Bridge over the Nanny river.*

have been out of place on the shaven head of one of the Village People. Or was it maybe a secret royalist thing, equally hidden? What was she doing here, anyway? It was a festival, called Filmex, of course, and had a British section among which my film was included. Was I secretly a British gay royalist? Like Kenneth Williams, in love with all the oohs and aahs and m'ladys and the curtseying and the hand kissing. Or was it quite simply that she seemed friendly, someone performing a rather tiresome task with genuine interest in this one, next in line? In which case it wasn't a sexual charge at all I was feeling, just an appreciation of this unexpected warmth. Was I that lonely, that any hint of warmth beneath the expected patina of good manners had an erotic tint? I was working my way through these rather complicated emotions anyway, when I got the news that my father had died.

Underneath that Same Bridge

He had been fishing with his grandchildren, among them my daughter Sarah, and felt the first tremors of a heart attack. He managed to get them to the shore, and gave up the ghost, very soon after. I often wonder was the Drogheda–Dublin train thundering over it at the time.

Gave up the ghost. What an odd phrase. Became the ghost might be a better one. But even that didn't happen. He basically died before we could finish our conversation. Strange, I know, and there was a lot unspoken between fathers and sons then, and probably still is. He told ghost stories. Delighted in them, the kinds of tales of horror that parents would frown on these days. About a coach drawn by headless horses, on the night of the Cleggan disaster. About a figure that haunted St Anne's Estate (an overgrown park next to our house) dressed in a tall stovepipe hat. For some reason heads were always important in his stories, whether severed or dressed in black, funereal stovepipe hats. This figure would warn anyone unlucky enough to encounter him that 'the day is for the living, the night is for the dead'. And these figures weren't only imaginary, residues of Edgar Allan Poe and late-night TV horror tales. When my younger sister, Dervil, was about nine or ten, he became convinced that she was accompanied by a poltergeist. A what, I can hear the question. A malignant spirit that hangs around young girls approaching puberty. Or mischievous, maybe, more than malignant. That rattles cupboards, misplaces familiar objects, leaves a garden rake, unaccountably, in the kitchen. He would find chapter and verse for the evidence of such creatures – or phenomena – in the literatures and anthropologies of other cultures. Whatever happened to this poltergeist I can't remember – it probably vanished around the time of her first boyfriend, but the absolute certainty that there was another dimension besides the observable stayed with me, and, I can only assume, remained with him. So when he was visited by the uninvited guest into the undiscovered infinite house, and when I heard, just after shaking Princess Anne's hand in the cinema in Los Angeles, and had to take the first plane home, I must have had two thoughts ringing round my head. The first was that he would have finally, I believe, taken fully to heart the film I had just made. It had everything he relished. Imaginary forests, small gingerbread houses dwarfed by the roots of enormous trees, wolves, visitations from beyond the grave and maybe even the poltergeists he was convinced hovered around his pubescent daughters. It was a fairy tale turned upside down and inside out. The second was that he would finally deliver the proof that he always wanted. He would haunt, if not me, then the house we all grew up in.

But there was, when I finally made it to the funeral home in Raheny, a kind of sere, clarifying absence. He was laid out in a coffin in one of those fake suburban living rooms, just down from the oddly named Middle Third. Maybe he had taken the Contemptible bus route to the Final Third. Dressed in a jacket and a twill shirt, and brown pants, though I may be wrong about that. The face as restful as I had ever seen it, a pair of glasses perched on the bridge of his cold nose. Whoever had placed those glasses, I had no idea, since he had no need of glasses now. The eyelids were closed and the brown eyes hidden. There came then a sense of lacerating emptiness.

There was grief, of course, too sudden to understand clearly. There must have been a service, in the church on St Gabriel's Road, a church I was never sure he believed in and which I don't remember the funeral mass. For somebody so convinced that the dead walked, on a parallel road to the living, there was a depressingly haphazard feeling to the choice of graveyard. On a slope, in Sutton, adjacent to Howth, with flattened gravestones, lying alongside the hole that had been dug by a small JCB, with its attendant operators, who I presume would be termed gravediggers. There was not even the dignity of a shovel or a gravestone that stood proud of the grass. Well, we were never a flamboyant or demonstrative family. But I remember thinking, as the coffin was lowered beneath its covering of green astroturf, now is your opportunity. Come on, haunt me.

That the haunting never came was disappointing, but not, I suppose, unexpected. I would lie awake at night, in whatever hotel or temporary flat I had ended up in, and wait for an unexplained hand on my arm. In the strange state of wanting to be terrified, wanting that childhood curtain of dread to descend, that all of the stories promised. It never came. The voice never resumed its instruction, its concerns that I was taking the wrong or the right path. And I realized that death, more than anything, is a rudely interrupted conversation.

When I came to make *The Crying Game*, I placed a carnival on the spit of land between the bridge and the sea, and devised a shot that tracked over the walkway, with the bridge in the foreground and the carnival beyond. The lens was a little too wide, and so the upper part of the bridge was distorted, at either end of the frame, which still upsets me whenever I see it.

When I came to make *Michael Collins* I used the bridge for a pivotal scene involving detective Ned Broy meeting his secret ally, Collins. They both held umbrellas, in a soft rain, which for some reason reminded me of Hokusai. An earlier version of the Drogheda to Dublin train thundered by.

They have destroyed the bridge by now, of course, since everything with a little bit of eccentricity and oddness has to go. But I can't be done with bridges. Something to do with crossing, transitions, from one state to another. My first published story, 'Last Rites', described a bridge that crossed from the Harrow Road to somewhere on Ladbroke Grove, over an endless jumble of railway tracks. When that bridge in turn was about to be consigned to history, a lady from Westminster Council got in touch about its preservation, wanting to erect a plaque of some kind. *Mona Lisa* opens with Bob Hoskins walking over Westminster Bridge, a package from Her Majesty's Prison Service in his hands. A crucial scene in which he questions the young Sammi Davis happens on the bridge to Waterloo Station, also now demolished, and the mess of rolling stock beneath it led in my mind all the way back to the bridge over Ladbroke Grove. With Roger Pratt, the cameraman, we pulled every second plank from the handrail so the evening sun would pour through and we could see the tracks better.

The Monsignor

Then there was the Golden Gate Bridge, over San Francisco Bay with which *Interview with the Vampire* begins and ends.

I had been offered the film by David Geffen, who had been trying to make the book by Anne Rice into a film for more than twenty years. He had a script by Anne herself, which was rich and gothic and extravagant but lacked so much of the book she herself had written. She called me to persuade me to do it, and in the course of the phone call told me that Lestat's favourite movie was *The Company of Wolves*. I was intrigued by this author who regarded her creation as a living creature, with favourite movies, books and rock and roll songs. So I read the novel again and was immediately entranced. By the atmosphere that you could almost inhale. By the saga of drenched, Catholic guilt that pervaded everything. By the curse of eternal life that Lestat had visited on his chosen one, Louis. By Claudia, the daughter they had turned in order to complete their vampiric family. It had everything, really, so much of human life seen through a cracked, metaphorical mirror, everything except what you would call a story. It was the worst kind of narrative for a film, a picaresque one. Lestat gives Louis the gift of eternal life and they bitch together, through the centuries. Like those eighteenth-century sagas about the getting of wisdom, except the promised wisdom and the anticipated peace never arrives. Still, if I could make the themes resonate through the centuries, of the loss of innocence and light, it could possibly be a vampire film like no other.

I asked David could I try my own hand at the script, and he said yes. I began and it almost wrote itself, so quickly I was embarrassed to tell David and Warners that I had finished. But I had to hand it over eventually, and they liked it so much they put it into immediate production. I was wary of studios, Hollywood, the demands of a huge and expensive production. I had been there before, and knew I worked best with an independent palette. I explained my concerns to David, and he made me an extraordinary promise. That whatever the budget, whatever the cast, whatever the scale of the film we would make, he would ensure I made it without interference, as an independent production. It was an offer I couldn't refuse, from a man who always kept his word.

The problem was the casting of Lestat. Brad Pitt had agreed to play Louis and somehow assumed Daniel Day-Lewis would be playing Lestat. It was an assumption shared by Anne, who had her own favourites for the casting of Lestat over the years. Everyone from Jeremy Irons to Rutger Hauer. I offered it to Daniel, who read it, and, as I expected, didn't want to play the character. He had confined himself to a wheelchair to play Christy Brown in *My Left Foot*. He would have had to sleep in a coffin for the entirety of this production, if he followed the same practice. So we had to move on.

David asked me if I wanted to meet Tom Cruise. Now a meeting like that is a kind of a trap, because you're damned if you do and damned if you don't. You can't really say no to the biggest star in the universe. So if you agree to meet, it says something. If you refuse to meet, it says something else. But I had always loved his performances, that cool commitment with which he held the centre of whatever picture he was in, from *The Outsiders* onwards. *A Few Good Men, Born on the Fourth of July* could only have been achieved by a real actor, as well as a star.

And anyway, what on earth was a star? So I drove out, to the rather unshowy house he had in Brentwood, and met one. My first impression was of a rather chilled, and again unshowy, perfection. I was buzzed in through a small, gated entrance. Waited on a terrace while another unshowy assistant poured me a glass of cold water. The assistant wore jeans and a white T-shirt, had one of those leather belts with a bum bag round his waist. Who knows what was inside it. Then Tom enters, again in jeans and a white T-shirt, but without the belted bag. So anything he needed would come from the assistant's bag.

He had the script, his lines outlined in a yellow or green felt pen, the way actors do. I could never work out whether that was that an aide-memoire or a guide to how much their part would occupy in the finished picture. But he seemed fascinated by the character, the strength, the absence of any moral compass whatsoever. I remembered as we talked something that Sean Penn had told me. Of all the young roustabouts of his generation, Cruise was the toughest, would never back down. I couldn't quite get that picture from the preternaturally polite young man beside me, but there was something. There was something eerily self-made even about his physique, his evident fitness. He hadn't got the body of an athlete. But he was an athlete. In any competition he had entered, there was no doubt whatsoever that he would win.

I left him with a strange feeling. I wasn't sure. Neither, evidently, was he. But I was unsettled. As, it turned out, was he. Because I got a call from David Geffen that night asking me to go back for another meeting. Tom evidently worked behind the scenes. In that strange ether where things are decided. Clipped phone calls, curt messages, polite exchanges in a freemasonry that worked out what was what. And then I understood.

In a subsequent novel, without much of the power of her first, Anne Rice had placed Lestat in Hollywood. In a gated mansion, down a discreet drive. He wasn't an actor, in this iteration, although he could have been. He was a rock and roll star.

I drove back out to Brentwood, back through the gated entrance. Sat down on the same terrace, to be given another bottled water by the same assistant. I was told Tom was out on a bike ride. I looked out on the hilly expanse around and had an image of him ascending them effortlessly, without any expense of sweat whatsoever. I was happy to wait. Because I finally got it. He had to live a life removed from the gaze of others. He had made a contract with the hidden forces, whatever they turned out to be. He had to hide in the shadows, even in the Hollywood sunlight. He would be eternally young. He was a star. He could well be Lestat.

He was also a superb actor, but that small fact got lost in the outrage that followed. Half of America, it seemed, had read Anne Rice's books and wanted a say in the casting of Lestat.

Anne herself took to the airwaves, saying that it was as if I had cast Edward G. Robinson as Rhett Butler. But she was wrong and was later big enough to admit it. I met a goth girl in a bar in New Orleans who insisted on showing me a tattoo on her butt of Rutger Hauer as Lestat. She was wrong, too. They were all wrong.

Brad Pitt was upset, but too much of a gentleman to make an issue of it. But the passivity of the role got him down, the unrelenting darkness. We shot for months in New Orleans, always at night. And now I was on the Golden Gate Bridge in San Francisco, again at night, trying to work out how to begin and end the film, when the chief of police roared up on a motorbike.

You're Irish, I'm Irish, he said. He wasn't, he was as American as the Harley he was riding, but I knew what he meant.

Anything you want in this city, just let me know.

And actually, oddly enough, there was. I remembered two of my father's cousins, from the other bridge, over the Nanny in Laytown. Probably with fishing rods in their hands. Walking the oozing mud in bare feet, pants rolled up around their ankles. Both devilishly handsome, dark-haired, a kind of Gene Kelly version of what my own father could have been. One of them was a priest, a monsignor, actually, and he flaunted a gold cigarette lighter, impossibly glamorous, a priest who lit his cigarette with gold that glittered.

There was a time, believe it or not, when priests could be glamorous. Or maybe that was only monsignors. The term monsignor was one I didn't fully understand but I knew it was in a different category from the dandruff-fringed parish priest who said mass in the old church down from the Nanny river.

The monsignor had a gold cigarette lighter which he displayed on the putting green, and wore not that housekeeper's funereal dress thing that most priests wore, but a close-fitting black suit that could have been worn by Frank Sinatra. More hair than Frank Sinatra, dark, Vaselined backwards so you could see the grid the comb threads had left. I'm sure he had a good handicap, too, although golf was never my thing. Anyway, I remember him, brother of Sonny and Sally, who I always thought of as one item. Sonny was married to Sally, of course, so the monsignor was his brother and the trio seemed to waft in a kind of Hollywood mist down the sand-blown streets that led to the golf and tennis courts. Auburn blown-back hair for Sally, and the dark, greased Italian style hair for the two brothers, one of them a monsignor.

He had gone to South America, I had heard, and in the ferment of liberation theology had left the priesthood and married – was it a nun? I could imagine them both in green fatigues with Kalashnikovs swung over their shoulders, him barely sweating in the torrid jungle, pausing by a tamarind tree, pulling out a pack of Lucky Strikes and offering one to her – who looked suspiciously like his sister-in-law from the Bettystown dunes – and lighting his and hers with – what else? – the same gold cigarette lighter. He has kept it! She accepts the barely perceptible flame, which has lost its amber glow in the fierce sunlight that pours down from the umbrella of leaves far, far above. Still, her Lucky Strike glows and she inhales, oblivious to the chattering of monkeys from the olive-fringed umbrella above. But is it the glow of the flame or the wisp of smoke above the glowing embers of tobacco that gives them away? No – the reflected flash of sunlight off the gold cigarette lighter. Of course. Why has he kept it? It's a lucky charm. He bought it in one of those stalls around St Peter's, or, even better, it was given to him on his ordination by my father's father's brother or my father's mother's sister and does it matter in the end? Because a fly buzzes past – not a fly, a mosquito, a cloud of mosquitos, and a rancid thing bigger than a bluebottle, bigger than many bluebottles, which has a deep-timbred buzzing all of its own. And he recognizes the sound, barely in time, throws his half-finished cigarette into the mulchy rainforest floor and pulls her to the ground, as the RPG flies past, exploding harmlessly into a nearby swamp. Maybe it kills a crocodile. They are both buried in mud, or maybe not mud, in the mulch of leaves which has a sweet, even syrupy smell and her cigarette has lost its burning tip and he reaches into his field pocket for the same gold cigarette lighter to do the gentlemanly thing once more. Lights it.

Anyway, I had an uncle who was a monsignor, who left the church for some reason in South America whose name was Jimmy or Peadar Kearns and I was on the Golden Gate Bridge preparing for the opening and closing shots of *Interview with the Vampire*. We had to close off one section of the bridge, so Tom Cruise could drive over it having drunk the blood of Christian Slater and the chief of police of the San Francisco area is beside me on his Harley-Davidson. It is the first time the bridge has been closed, even in part, for any kind of motion-picture shoot and it is a very big deal. He asks me again. Anything he can do to help, over the few days I'm in town.

And that's when I remember the monsignor. He had retired, I had been told, from the jungles of Ecuador, or from the streets of Quito, probably to a seminary, converted into a social housing project (with or without the nun? I had no idea) and was now running a bar in the Tenderloin district of San Francisco. And even the name Tenderloin had that odd hint of glamour – or was it danger? – that the gold cigarette lighter brought with it and the imagined Ecuadorian jungle.

So this kindly, white-haired chief of police on his Harley, on the Golden Gate Bridge, takes down my phone number, with his notes. Ex-monsignor. Bar. Tenderloin. Give me twenty-four hours.

I shot the scene the next night. Christian Slater drives over the moonlit bridge, in an open-topped car. He places the tape of his interview in the deck, presses play and hears Brad Pitt's voice come over the speakers.

Most of all I longed for death…

A hand grabs the interviewer's neck, pulls him flat. Lestat, of course, who sinks his teeth in. Takes the wheel.

Oh, Louis, Louis, still whining.

Have you heard enough? I've had to listen to that for centuries.

And it was odd, in the end, the way the actors' approach to their roles mirrored the roles themselves. Louis, the reluctant vampire, played by Brad, the reluctant actor.

He had a hard time. Forgive me, Brad.

Lestat, who toys with that very reluctance, played by Tom, who never let a part defeat him.

As Stephen Woolley put it, it was like having Elvis and Frank Sinatra in the same film.

I go back to my hotel room. Sleep, always like a vampire, through the day.

A phone call wakes me up. It is the chief of police, within the requisite twenty-four hours. He gets immediately to the point.

Ex-monsignor. Runs a bar. Tenderloin and downtown San Francisco environs.

I've found seventeen, he tells me.

Now I'm sure not all of them looked like Frank Sinatra, carried a gold cigarette lighter, married a nun after getting swept away by the heady winds of liberation theology, but one of them would have to be him. But what puzzled me most was the number. Seventeen. It puzzled the chief of police as well, so he began to make enquiries. And, of course, he found that most of them didn't want to be contacted, by Irish relatives in particular. Many of them could have been gay, had entered mature relationships, married, even, gay and straight, and I hoped none of them had left the church for more dubious reasons, cases pending back in colleges at home, all of the sad detritus of Irish Catholicism. Anyway, the chief of police pursued his enquiries, which I began to regret I had set in motion. And one Friday evening – I was due to leave, I remember, on the Saturday – he told me that an ageing cleric, who had the key to this diaspora, would be calling me. So the phone rang and a voice out of the more realistic memories of my childhood came on. It had lost none of its West of Ireland rise and fall of complaint. I was back behind a desk in a Christian Brothers school, my bare knees banging off the screws underneath. Because I recognized that voice. It had nothing to do with gold cigarette lighters, or close-fitting Frank Sinatra suits. It wore a soutane and had a leather concealed in the inner folds of the swishing black serge.

Who are you enquiring about, it asked.

My uncle, I replied. Peadar, or Jimmy Kearns.

And why?

He's an ex-priest, I told him. Or an ex-monsignor. He runs a bar in San Francisco. One, I have been told, among seventeen.

There was another pause. He was the keeper of secrets, this old gentleman, and I had to assure him I was looking for none of them. I was making a film in San Francisco and just wanted to reacquaint myself with a piece of my more innocent childhood.

Where's he from?

Roscommon.

I remembered the photo of the accordion-playing schoolteacher.

Where in Roscommon?

And I had to rack my brains. Boyle, I remembered, was where my father was born. But maybe not the Kearnses. And suddenly a name popped into my head. A kind of Grecian name, with a tincture of myth to it. Something to do with elves. Much more romantic than Boyle.

Elphin?

And even the name triggered some kind of release. He exhaled, gave me the address of a Tenderloin bar.

I had to leave the next lunchtime. Take a plane back to Los Angeles. But I had the car swing by the bar, in the early morning. Entered one of those working-class watering holes, where a young kid was swabbing the counter amid last night's beer fumes. I asked for Peader Kearns, brother of Sonny. Or was the name Jimmy?

Mister Kearns, I was told was away for the weekend, would be back on Monday.

Does he, I asked the kid, still have a gold cigarette lighter?

He looked confused. You want a light? he asked. No smoking in here.

I had so many questions. Does he still look like Frank Sinatra in a clerical collar? Did he wander the jungles of Ecuador in an outfit like Che Guevara or Daniel Ortega? Saving his missus, the defrocked nun, from incoming RPGs?

And what about Elphin? Were there elves there? Or was it a secret Grecian glade, mystically transported to the boglands of Roscommon? And by the way, were there tender loins in the Tenderloin?

So many questions, but the car was waiting. We were shooting in London next.

So I left a note and drove back over the Golden Gate Bridge to the airport.

The Dark Gift

The film had been made in an insane glare of publicity. Anne Rice had very publicly railed against the casting of Tom Cruise. We had made it almost entirely at night, in a black-draped New Orleans, Paris and London. Whole streets had to be shrouded in curtains, to occlude any possibility of images getting out and adding to the media frenzy. We lived by night, for months. But the heart of the frenzy centred round the issue of sexuality. Would I, would Geffen (himself a publicly gay man) would Warners somehow occlude, mute or blur the homoerotic elements of the book? Which was interesting, actually, given my experience with the script itself.

The first script that David Geffen had sent me, by Anne, was theatrical, flamboyant, picaresque, but almost utterly devoid of any sense of what we would now call 'transgression'. It was avoiding something darker, something deeper, something metaphorical. I read the book, and its sequels, and asked to write my own version. (Because of the complexity of WGA agreements with the studios, I never got a credit. A director (or 'production executive') who rewrites an existing script has to prove they wrote something approaching 90 per cent of a screenplay to be credited.) But that, in the end, didn't matter. I fell in love with the book, and wanted to write a script that did it justice. So I could make a film that did it justice.

But the strange thing is, there was no sexual content. There was homoerotic subtext, everywhere. There was bondage, there was dominance, there was a lifelong (infinite, actually) attachment to male physical beauty. There was the dilemma of two men, fatefully bound together, a family in everything but their ability to conceive. So they make a vampire of an orphan child. And the subsequent presumptions about the filmed version, that it somehow diminished the sexual content of the novel, was beyond wrong. It was lazy. It could only be made by someone who had never read the book.

Drink from me and live forever.

These vampires never fucked. They killed, in a frenzy of hunger. They created companions in a frenzy of need. They were outside time. Outside morality. Outside sex. But, above all, they were lonely.

Which was a wonderful theme and a wonderful irony. If they could have fucked, they wouldn't have been lonely. Blood was the substitute for sex. Hence the dilemma, the dreadful attraction of what Lestat called 'the dark gift'.

Anne was smart and generous enough to recognize this when she saw the finished film. She wrote an article, and paid for a front page of *Variety* to say how much she loved it.

So to anyone who says the film avoided what she wrote, I would say: read the book.

Evergreen

The odd thing is, I didn't take to *Michael Collins* that much. My mother was a De Valera admirer which is odder still, given all of the rumours of the London post office and the presumed acquaintance with my grandmother. Would he have even noticed her own mother, behind the burnished brass rods of the small booth she had to occupy, a little like her own prison as she sorted the mail that he would deliver, on his bicycle, of course, round the great houses of Kensington and Chelsea? Again, there is no knowing. But my first real introduction to the Cuchulain of Irish freedom was through David Puttnam, who approached me after my first film, *Angel*, was released.

Initially he sent me the manuscript of a novel called *Cal*, by Bernard MacLaverty, a rather moving tale of an IRA hanger-on who had driven a car that was used in the assassination of an RUC man, and, transfixed by guilt, fell into a relationship with his widow. I proposed a variation on the simple and effective story, as I couldn't really help myself. Which went like this: that far from having ruined this beautiful widow's life, the hero finds out that, quite by accident, he had been her inadvertent saviour. The RUC man was a brutal and abusive

Michael Collins – *crowd scene.*

force in her life, the marriage an obscenity, and the bloody assassination, while repellent and unconscionable, provided her with the only possible release from an intolerable situation. I tend to do those things: ruin a perfectly decent sentimental narrative by twisting the narrative possibilities into something more grotesque. Or something that suits my own sensibility.

David, very wisely, turned these possibilities down and made a film that was as true to the novel as it possibly could be. But, some months afterwards, he asked me to consider a script on the life of Michael Collins.

My only image of Collins was of a militaristic figure on the cover of a book by Frank O'Connor, called *The Big Fellow*, dressed in a green army uniform, gazing upwards in an olive-green officer's cap. That one was on my father's bookshelf. It was probably as ubiquitous in Irish homes as the framed picture of the pope and of Éamon de Valera. But I began to read. I went into the loveliest room in the world, in the Irish National Library, borrowed two enormous hardbacked tomes by a man called Piaras Béaslaí. When I had finished these two volumes, I liked Collins even less. A kind of saint of violence, devoutly Catholic. A Garibaldi, or dare I say it, a possible Mussolini of the Irish revolution. But then I began to realize, that this was more than the actual Collins. The sanctimonious tone of the Gaelic League, the hagiographic Catholicism, the heroic appeal to a world of ancient Irish sagas.

There was something more complicated there, in this figure. For one thing, during six brief years of his life, from 1916 to 1922, he was the pivotal figure in the conflict, from the suicidal events of 1916, through the War of Independence and its aftermath, a civil war. There was a hard-headed realism about this guy, who could build an army to run that ragged conflict against the British Empire, and when he had achieved the best deal he could, attempt to disestablish it. There was the tragedy, of course, of his early death. We had been brought up with one version of Irish history. 'Four Green Fields', the song and the concept, blood-soaked martyrs and the Provisional IRA in the North of Ireland were perpetuating that version. Collins had run that race, and abandoned it, more than eighty years before.

I did some more research and began to write. I wrote fast. I still lived in a house in Bray at the time and had been given the use of one of those early computers. It used a printer with continuous stationery with those sprocket perforations on the side. To print one page, it had to be torn off from the others so I gave up on the printing and just kept going. I eventually finished the script and I hit print and watched, appalled, as the room filled up with paper. All I could think of was the broom filling the room with water in *The Sorcerer's Apprentice*. I had to catch a plane to London and stuffed the typescript into a black plastic bag and caught a taxi. I untangled it in the plane or the hotel room and read what I had written.

It wasn't bad, I had to admit, and the possibility of dramatizing, through one character, the events of 1916, the guerrilla war that followed it, the treaty negotiations and the Civil War was an intriguing one. I don't remember whether Mr Puttnam agreed. I do remember he asked for some illumination of Collins's early life. Is it something to do with the form of the biopic or the influence of Sigmund Freud that everything has to be seen through the prism of a childhood memory? Maybe it's Orson Welles's fault, that Kane child with the toboggan in the snow. Anyway, did I write those scenes or not? I must have, because I was eventually allowed to make the film, I shot them.

David had a deal with Warner Bros. at the time who read the script and put it into a vault and forgot all about it. David moved on to a stint at Columbia, among other things. I probably went back to Bray and tried to forget all about it.

It was hard, though. The story had such resonance. Those pivotal events, in six brief years of a young man's life. He was thirty-one when he died. Didn't even make it to a Christ-like thirty-three. It had resonance for others, too. Michael Cimino came and went, touring the country in search of locations. And that thought was intriguing. The eye that had made *The Deer Hunter* and *Heaven's Gate* applied to our own War of Independence? But he was probably more interested in Salvatore Giuliano and went on to make his own version of Francesco Rosi's masterpiece, *Salvatore Giuliano*, as *The*

Sicilian. And now that I think of it, there were some parallels, more fruitful than the comparisons with Garibaldi.

I didn't get to make the film, nor did Michael Cimino. The next attempt was by Kevin Costner, who had taken to a script written by an Irish journalist, Eoghan Harris. An extensive biography came out, written by another Irish journalist/ historian, Tim Pat Coogan. The figure of Collins was gaining resonance as the distance to the events grew greater. Maybe it reflected a need to reassess some sanctified versions of Irish history. But the subject was public domain, and nobody owned it. So whoever got to make it first, good luck to them.

But none of them succeeded. And now I had made a film for Warner Brothers, that hallowed studio which had bought my script more than twenty years ago. *Interview with the Vampire* had proved a substantial hit and Bob Daly and Terry Semel, the two wise and terrifying chairmen of the enterprise, asked me into their office and wondered what I wanted to do next.

You have a script of mine, I told them, called – and I had to make an effort to remember the title – *Evergreen* and I would love to make it.

Evergreen? they asked. A *How Green Was My Valley* kind of thing?

No, I said. The title is ironic. It's more of a Salvatore Giuliano kind of thing. About Michael Collins, who led the War of Independence from England.

Bob Daly was Irish. Or Irish American. He knew the name. Terry Semel didn't. But they had the power, these men, and that other mysterious quality, chutzpah, to push this thing through.

These Irish/English-type pictures, Terry says to me, make fifteen to twenty million dollars tops.

There are fifty million Americans who claim Irish ancestry.

And I'm one of them, said Bob. And I know, not all of them go to the pictures.

But they promised to think about it. And David Geffen promised to help.

I had met Liam Neeson on the set of *Excalibur*. And I had seen him on stage at the Gate in Brian Friel's *Translations*. A huge physical presence, playing an unlettered character called Doalty. I will never forget him turning to the British officer in the hedge-schoolhouse, saying casually, 'Tell him his whole camp's on fire'. I told Liam I was writing the script at the time, and that if I ever got to make it, I would make it with him. It was now more than twenty years later. Was he too old? He had just played Oskar Schindler in *Schindler's List*, so it was obvious he wasn't.

Julia Roberts called. She had read the script, and spent her spare time in Ireland. She wanted to meet.

And here was the old star dilemma. The minute Warner Brothers heard of it, the picture was assured. And so I met her, in the screening room of the ICM building. She loved the script. Loved the part. She would do it for nothing. She was sweetness itself. I said yes.

The rumour that the film would happen spread like wild-fire in Ireland. There was talk of a ceasefire in the North. A 'negotiated peace process'. For some reason, the idea of Collins seemed to spread the odour of a new beginning, a reassessment. Political realities that had been set in stone for generations were crumbling. I began the recces, the sketching out of sets, photographing Dublin streets to see which of them could serve to recreate the city of the 1920s, with Tony

Pratt, the designer. To my amazement, there were still whole streetscapes intact. If we could manage the traffic, block out the street signs, turn the tarmac into cobblestone, we could have a fair shot at recreating the city that Collins cycled through. (In fact, if you compare the city we photographed with whatever of it remains today, you would build a special prison for planning officers, city councillors and developers.) But O'Connell Street was, and still is, a mess. The only solution was to build the General Post Office, the headquarters of the 1916 rebellion, on the site of Grangegorman, a derelict mental hospital. We could build the façade of the GPO, quite a section of O'Connell Street and a portion of the various streets adjacent to it, among them Abbey Street. We could reproduce Clery's, with its famous clock. The only problem was that we would have to manipulate the geography. Abbey Street would lead directly onto the pillars of the General Post Office, which is not accurate. But it might provide an even better perspective than existed in actuality.

I gradually came to realize I had fallen into an awkward situation. Everybody had an opinion about the script, on the casting, on the outcome of the film itself. It was as if I had been commissioned to sculpt a national monument, and had to obey all of the rules of monumental sculpture. A raised hoof means one thing, a pointed spear another. Every small gesture I made would be interpreted and more than likely misinterpreted. The problem was that nobody had commissioned me. I had pushed the film through the Warners bureaucracy and it was a matter of luck that they were letting me do it. They didn't care that much about political niceties. They just didn't want to lose money. They had a large distribution enterprise in England to keep nice with, so neither did they want controversy. But having made the decision to back the film, they would stick by it.

But this film could no more avoid controversy than butter could avoid flies. Crowds began visiting the Grangegorman set even before it was completed. The script, which nobody outside the set had read, incidentally, and which I was continuously rewriting, was analysed on early morning talk shows and TV specials. Academics, North and South, got in on the act. And I began to realize the truth of Gore Vidal's dictate: never give up the opportunity to have sex or go on television. Whatever about sex, academics and journalists loved their television. And the whole frenzy of argument was complicated by the fact that there was a very real drama taking place in the North of Ireland, which paralleled the drama in Collins's own political life. He had tried, and failed, to entirely 'decommission' (to use the contemporary parlance,) the irregular army he had built. Would Martin McGuinness, Gerry Adams, Gerry Kelly, meet the same fate? If there was tragedy in the arc of his life, and there was, it was a tragic arc that still had resonance.

I was faced with the dilemma of anyone who dramatizes history. What to put in, what to take out. What amount of telescoping of the actual facts is permissible? I had to reduce the events of Bloody Sunday into seven or eight minutes of screen time. I used an armoured vehicle on the pitch of Croke Park so the event would not last an afternoon (as the actual shootings did). I merged the characters of Dick McKee and Peadar Clancy, who were done to death after Collins's assassinations of the Cairo Gang. I could have changed the name, but grew fatally attached to the mispronunciation of it by Charles Dance's character, in the shadows of the Castle gates.

Good night, boy.

It's Broy, sir. Broy.

So Broy it had to be.

Authenticity

The core of the arguments about authenticity were simple. Did this happen, did that happen, did what happened in the film have any correspondence with what happened in reality. For the Treaty debates, which were shot in a library in Trinity College (they actually happened in a medical lecture room in Newman House, which even then was the premises of University College Dublin) every word I placed into the actor's mouths were words from the record. This led to certain awkwardnesses since the dialogue of the delegates at the time was almost novelettish in its sense of high drama. Collins bellowed, when Dev led his deputies out of the premises, 'Traitors! Traitors all!', a line that Liam Neeson delivered, but that lacked to me, anyway, any sense of character, and, yes, the aura of authenticity. But should the apparent authenticity be allowed to triumph over the actual?

So it was odd to hear, in subsequent years, from the mouths of successive government ministers, from even a Taoiseach and a president or two, lines attributed to Michael Collins that I had written for my own film. One of the stranger ironies of historical authenticity, maybe. The fictional lines become part

The Treaty Debates.

of the historical record. At the annual commemorations of his assassination, at Béal na Bláth, they have become almost obligatory and ritual quotations:

'Give us the future. We've had enough of your past. Give us our country back. To live in. To grow in. To love.'

But apologies to all. He never said that, never wrote that. I did.

I took a simple approach to the Collins drama. I used the template of the gangster films *White Heat* and *The Public Enemy*, Howards Hawks's *Scarface* to draw together as many of the historical events of the period as I could.

This led to certain misinterpretations. A car bomb scene in Dublin Castle, which could have come straight from a silent movie or Orson Welles's *Touch of Evil*, was seen as a snide reference to car bombs in the Northern conflict that was just winding down. I found this upsetting, since I had returned to

Dublin in 1982 to attend the funeral of my wife's relative who had been killed in the Dublin bombings of that year. Every person on that boat – this was before Ryanair – was coming back for the funeral of a family member killed and cursed the country that was dragging them home.

I suppose nobody can get everything right, in particular when the drama you are making parallels so eerily the drama that was happening to the north of you, across the border. Had we finished the film, or not yet begun it when the Canary Wharf bomb threatened to wreck the whole peace process? I remember sitting in a screening room in New York, with Chris Menges and Stephen Woolley, and hearing the news. It threatened to wreck the film, too. But we somehow, with the support of the studio if nothing else, managed to keep going.

It was an epic experience to have a whole city placed at your disposal, to have crowds in their thousands willing to participate. To have Alan Rickman in his first appearance as De Valera deliver his 'Rivers of Blood' speech on a stand on a rebuilt O'Connell Street in front of four thousand extras.

I had a strange memory of the same De Valera. I had stood with my father and heard him speak, a tall, frail and elderly figure speaking in Irish to a crowd outside the actual GPO.

I also remembered his actual funeral. It was raining, as it always seemed to be on O'Connell Street, and most of the crowds were gathered round the windows of television stores, watching the funereal event behind them on TV. There was an odd metaphorical resonance to the scene, which I wrote about in a story called 'A Love': 'We walked outside then and the brass music became a deafening thud. We walked slowly down the street, we couldn't talk, the music was so loud. I bought a newspaper at the corner of Abbey Street and saw a headline about the funeral that was crawling along beside us. We passed a TV sales shop where a crowd of people were staring at a white screen, staring at the death being celebrated behind them.'

There was an entirely different film to be made about De Valera but nobody was going to give me the money to make it. It would have involved prevarication, conflicts with Churchill, who described conversations with him as akin to 'picking mercury up with a fork'. Alan Rickman, who caught his intonations beautifully, would have loved to do it. I can imagine Alan playing his re-entry into the Dáil, swearing the hated Oath of Allegiance while concealing with the Bible the text he was swearing allegiance to.

'I said: "I am not prepared to take an oath. I am not going to take an oath. I am prepared to put my name down in this book in order to get permission to go into the Dáil, but it has no other significance."'

This strange figure, from Bruree in County Limerick by way of Spain and New York, with his predilection for mathematics, Gaelic games and Catholicism. They were all Catholic, anyway, it seemed to go with republicanism the way pasta went with Italian cuisine, the way potatoes went with Irish stew, but I suppose the basic question was, would it have been different if Collins had lived? I have to convince myself it would. Some different resolution in the Six Counties. The smaller island standing with the larger, in the Second World War. Collins would never have visited the German ambassador to express his regrets on the death of their Führer, as De Valera did in May 1945. Even if neutrality had prevailed, he would have had more sense.

Did De Valera have a hand in Collins's death? Probably not, but he could have prevented it. Did he have a nervous breakdown in the aftermath? I believe so, absolutely. And we all had to live inside it.

The obvious place to showcase the Collins film would have been the Cannes Film Festival. But I was worried about the swarm of British journalists on the Croisette. We offered it to Venice and they accepted it, and it won two Golden Lions, one for the film and one for Liam Neeson's performance.

Julian Senior, the head of Warner Brothers in England, was a huge supporter of the film and began showing it to journalists. One, from the *Daily Telegraph*, began an immediate campaign against the film, writing three editorials, demanding that Warner Bros. cancel the film's release 'forthwith'. And I presume that meant immediately.

Julian showed it to Garret FitzGerald, a former head of government and the prime initiator of a previous attempt at peace, the Anglo-Irish Agreement. Garret wrote a response in the *Irish Times* that was considered rather praiseworthy.

The Special Branch came out to my house and showed me how to check the chassis of my car for hidden explosives. Things were definitely getting hot.

So maybe it was inevitable that when the film came out the whole of Ireland came to see it. It broke box office records. It was released in America, and, as Bob Daly said, there may be fifty million Irish Americans, but they don't always go to the movies

These Irish-English pictures, as Terry Semel said, they do fifteen to twenty million dollars, tops.

I suppose we met their expectations.

I was flying back from New York and happened to be sitting

beside the same Garret FitzGerald. He cut an elegant, elderly figure, in his three-piece suit, but suffered from diabetes, and showed me how he could extract blood from his fingers to monitor his blood sugar levels. I thanked him for the article he had written, for his considered, genuine opinion, which had gone some way towards changing the fractious conversations about my film.

And that reminds me, he said, I must send in an invoice, I still haven't been paid

By the *Irish Times*? I asked him.

No, he said. By Warner Brothers.

The Butcher Boy

They asked me, what do you want to do next? I had bought the rights to Pat McCabe's *The Butcher Boy* and met him by the ramparts in Killiney. A small swimming place with one of those concrete bathing shelters above a few steps leading into the Irish Sea. I swam while Pat, wearing a combat jacket, hung around the shadows of the shelter, the way Flann O'Brien's De Selby might have done while thinking of St Augustine in the underwater cave below. Or the way my paedophile might have done, in another shelter, long, long ago, by the Bull Wall. Maybe he was De Selby. Pat was definitely the more realistic, rural inheritor of the voice of Flann O'Brien. He knew the same world I did, I could immediately tell that. In fact, he had written a book that had such immediate familiarity to people, that they felt only they could understand it. The voice of Francie Brady resonated inside many heads the way the voice of Holden Caulfield did, in *The Catcher in the Rye*. But it was a voice. And it was a galaxy far far away from anything Warner Brothers had ever done, or should ever do.

But I asked Pat to write a script. I paid for the first draft myself. He came back with another version of the story, a parallel version, which he has, in many ways, been writing ever since. I had to tell him after I'd read it that I was quite attached to the original book. The voice had totally vanished, for one thing. He had heard that voiceover was anathema to movies. I reminded him of *A Clockwork Orange*, and asked him would he mind if I had a go.

We were working on the edit of *Interview with the Vampire*, I remember, in Dean Street in Soho, and I had a small room to the back with a tiny balcony that overlooked Wardour Street. I would sit there between views of the edit and work on Pat's book. It had the extraordinary effect of bringing me back to my fifties childhood. Clontarf in 1959 must be as far away as possible from Clones in Co. Monaghan at the same time, but all of the irrationality of the period, the world where imaginary beings had the same purchase and reality as beings that existed, came back to me. Do you reject the Devil and all his works? We do, the dirty bastard. The book, that seemed unfilmable to many, had that kind of reality for me.

I finished the script, driven by Francie Brady's voiceover from a mental hospital in later life, about the Ireland he remembered from his youth which was itself a mental hospital, and Pat liked it. And the head of production of Warner Brothers was asking what I wanted to do next.

The more I told them this project wasn't for them, the more they wanted it. So I found myself in the extraordinary position of making this eccentric, wayward film for a Hollywood studio.

It was about boyhood, so I needed an extraordinary boy. I found three of them, in a small school in Killeshandra, near Clones, where the book was set. They would fly with the film, none of them had acted before and Eamonn Owens, who played the lead, had never been inside a cinema.

I had him read the script with his brother Kieran and his classmate Alan Boyle. I followed Eamonn then, with a video camera, around the locations the book described in the small town. Any awareness of me or the camera fell away and barely reappeared in the course of a long and complicated production. The strange immediacy you get from non-actors became the norm. I had been there before, of course, with Sarah Patterson in *The Company of Wolves*, Jaye Davidson in *The Crying Game*. It's an effect that is almost impossible to describe. Every take is for the first time. Nothing can really be repeated. It brings alive the Godardian principle, that film never stills or captures time, it somehow releases it. You never step in the same river twice, because by the time you come to say Take Two, the whole river has changed.

The book was considered unfilmable, which for me was part of the attraction. The fascination of what's difficult, as Yeats called it. There was the perspective, a child's vision, and we now had the child. There the town, which made up the universe the child lived in. Clones, near the border with the North, was where the book was set, and as Eamonn Owens provided the face, the physique and the performance, the town became a set. The 'Troubles' had meant the town was bypassed as a traffic hub, so it was little changed since the sixties. There was the child's imagination, which meant the town would be realistic one moment and fantastical the next

I had Stephen Rea play his father, the adult Francie, and become his voice. There was nothing literary about that voice. It was straight out of comic strips, tales of Billy Bunter and

Desperate Dan by way of Flash Gordon, and immediately demanded a style of acting that I couldn't describe, but was immediately apparent to me by its absence. I may have offended one or two actors, friends of mine, in the process. One was playing a kindly Christian Brother, but the tone was wrong. I asked him to repeat the same lines, wearing an alien fly head that I had designed for a fantasy sequence, and suddenly, magically, it became right.

I had to cast the Virgin Mary as a child would have imagined her. I considered various options. Making one of those stiff blue and white statues begin to move. Bringing Marilyn Monroe alive through visual effects and having her leap from the television straight into his imagination. Marilyn, her blonde tresses covered by the blue Blessed Virgin Mary shawl.

Then I thought of Sinéad O'Connor.

She had once been asked to play Joan of Arc, she told me, by Kathryn Bigelow, and would happily put the energy she had wasted into playing what she called the BVM. In fact she collected statues of the same BVM. Tall, etiolated, triangular mouldings of chalk, with the hands clasped on the chest, or spread out with the stiff blue folds of the chalk cloth falling away towards the floor. She had collected some of them from abandoned churches, and maybe even from the Magdalene home in which she spent a fair few months of her adolescence. So she played the BVM dressed in the same blue robes, in front of a blue screen with the same childlike simplicity. She could appear to the distressed Francie in a bog full of half-cut turf, in the screen of a broken television, on the wall of a psychiatrist's office. She could even share his argot. Ah Francie, for fuck's sake. Joe still loves you.

I showed the finished film to Billy Gerber, the head of production at Warner Brothers at the time, who had insisted they could not only make it, but release it properly. He sat at the back of the theatre after the screening, stunned. There was a long silence, which I broke by asking, what do you want to do, Billy, preview it? He answered, how the fuck do you preview that?

They previewed it eventually, in front of the usual invited audience on the Warner Brothers lot. The results on the test cards were all over the place. Those who loved it absolutely loved it, those who hated it hated it with equal passion. And to their credit, the studio never asked for any cuts. They could have torn it to shreds, in their efforts to make it amenable to an American audience. I had shot it in the accents of the Irish borderlands, comprehensibility was an obvious issue, but the film was too far beyond their comprehension to attempt any of the usual fixes. So they left it, and me, alone.

It was released and played well in Ireland, England, Europe, screened at the Berlin Festival and won several prizes. By the time the US release came about, several independents were begging to take it on. A film about a mesmerically disturbed boy who kills his next-door neighbour with a stun gun and chops up her body with a butcher's axe, in a country where high school shootings had become the norm, needed special handling. Warners were paradoxically proud of the film, though and didn't want to give it up.

And maybe that's what studios are for. To help you make these things, not to understand them.

Sarah and Stanley

I was scouting locations for a film in Massachusetts, looking for an abandoned mental hospital. So many location scouts seem to involve empty mental hospitals and prisons, factories gone to ruin, deconsecrated churches. Huge arenas of decay in which you can build whatever sets you need, blow them up, tear them down and maybe even set your own production offices somewhere inside them. Our production offices in this one were quite presentable, though, in a small town called Northampton. My daughter Sarah was working as my assistant, lucky me, and when I came back, covered in the grime of wherever I'd been, she told me I had received a phone call.

From who?

Stanley Kubrick.

It was truly a voice from the past. And I asked her what did he say?

He said, hello Sarah.

He knew your name?

He did.

He remembered you?

He seemed to.

From that phone call in Bray, all those years ago. How strange, I thought.

What did he say?

He said, Sarah, you're going to have to ask Neil to use his second choice for that little girl.

That little girl.

I had cast an adorable girl who had played the daughter of Tom Cruise and Nicole Kidman in *Eyes Wide Shut*. Her mother had told me she had finished shooting a year ago.

And then I remembered, he had called about two years before that again, to ask about Tom Cruise.

I had told him he was a very good actor.

He had better be, he said. Because he's not a star for his personality.

But how did he remember Sarah's name? And how did he know I had a second choice?

My first assistant director, the gentlemanly Patrick Clayton, had worked as his assistant on *2001* and *Barry Lyndon*.

When I cast the same girl, he said, he'll never let her go.

So I asked the mother to check her contract. She told me it had long expired.

Patrick, who had been a silent witness at that legendary lunch when Mr Kubrick asked Ryan O'Neal to get his leg cut off for *Barry Lyndon*.

The titular character survives the duel with Lord Bullingdon with a half-severed leg.

Mr Kubrick tells Patrick he has an issue he needs to discuss with Mr O'Neal. Would Patrick kindly invite him for lunch in his trailer?

Patrick walks to Mr O'Neal's trailer and tells him Mr

Kubrick would like to join him in his, Mr Kubrick's trailer, for lunch. Mr O'Neal is pleased, even honored, to accept.

Patrick walks back to Mr Kubrick's trailer and tells him Mr O'Neal would be happy to have lunch. Mr Kubrick asks Patrick to join them as well.

Patrick, who knows his place in the hierarchy of things, is surprised and a little uncomfortable, but has to agree.

And at the lunch, Mr Kubrick addresses the shot where Barry is seen in bed after the amputation.

Ryan O'Neal raises his eyebrows.

Yes?

Well, I've done a series of tests. With a double who has his leg tied behind him and a prosthetic stump attached to his knee.

And?

It doesn't work. The device can be seen from any angle.

OK.

I tried removing it optically. Again, it's impossible. We can get rid of the leg, but the stump is now the problem.

And?

I've contacted a very good clinic in Switzerland. The best, apparently. We can fly you there after shooting on Friday, redo the schedule to give you time for recovery and have an ambulance waiting to take you back to shoot the scene.

Recovery from what?

The operation.

What operation, Mr Kubrick?

To remove your leg. Just below the knee.

You're asking me to get my leg cut off for this film?

Well, I don't know what else to do. Maybe you have another solution?

Was he serious? Patrick couldn't tell. Even Ryan O'Neal couldn't tell. Why was he invited to be a witness? So he could tell the story to others? So it would become part of the legend? Mr Kubrick kept his reasons to himself.

But his first assistant director, who was now mine, knew one thing. He will never let her go.

I called back the number he had left with Sarah and got a production assistant.

Mr Kubrick is busy at present, but I'll tell him you called.

He didn't call back. But almost everyone else did. And I realized that Stanley, although he rarely left the house in St Albans, maintained telephone relationships with film-makers all over the world. Steven Spielberg, all the heads of DreamWorks, and, eventually, Bob Daly and Terry Semel of Warner Brothers. Everyone of note in the US called me, apart from the president, Bill Clinton. Nobody wanted to upset Stanley.

Least of all me.

I spoke with the mother. She begged me not to send her daughter back. She threatened lawsuits if I did.

I called every number I could find for Stanley. He was never there.

Then, one Sunday morning, I think it was, Sarah got another call. Handed the phone to me.

I'm sorry about all of this, Neil. I just don't know what to do. I have streets closed off, shops being dressed. The actors flying back. Doing reshoots next week.

It was oddly touching. Like talking to a film student. Or a first-time director. The world's greatest cineaste, in a genuine panic.

Or, like talking to an ersatz father, whom you had unknowingly displeased.

He had many relationships with directors, I would learn. Mostly from that telephone in St Albans. Were they all looking for a father to please?

I said of course, Stanley. I'm sorry, too.

And I used my second choice.

Was she visible in the reshoots? I hope so. He died six days after showing Warners his final cut.

The Virus

The Nuart is a small cinema on the way from West Hollywood to Santa Monica. I often drove past it while trying to find somewhere to walk, because walking, as everyone knows, is a problem in LA. You can walk, but you have to drive to do it. To place your feet on the ground, be it an overheated street corner or the kind of scrub you find in the runnels around Mullholland. And the experience can be quite special, particularly the Mullholland one. To see the entire Valley spread below you, or the spikes of Hollywood and downtown, Century City and the Pacific beyond while seeing an actual coyote scurry through the undergrowth is an experience you won't, needless to say, get anywhere else, and a unique one. The combination of urban sprawl under a curtain of brown smog and the kind of wilderness you find in yet to be developed real estate – for everything in Los Angeles is real estate, even nature in the wild. Undeveloped real estate, as in wilderness, or former real estate, which transitions back to wilderness with dystopian speed.

I might have loved and hated Los Angeles, but I never shared the contempt for it that Easterners and Europeans

274

prided themselves in. Even the enormous grid of the city, seen from a descending plane, the gridded suburbs, smaller hub cities, the dried up river running in between, all underneath the amber smog that hungover everything like a – well, like a hangover – had something, to use an LA term, awesome about it. Awesome in its uncaring hugeness, it futurity, in its contempt for the judgement of others. Passing the Hustler building on the way in from the airport, which was shaped like a cylindrical trash bin of the kind that I would find sitting close to my door in the Sunset Marquis Hotel. There was a period when hotel trash bins had quite a pleasing, cylindrical design and I could imagine the architect hired by whoever owned Hustler at the time, and it had to be Larry Flynt, sitting in his office, glancing down at the paper bin by his desk and saying, will that shape do, Mr Flynt? I would later find out that Flynt only bought the building from Western Union, but it made a Hustler kind of statement, the entire cladding of oversized paper bin, windows and all, being a discreet brown. A colour that may have taken its inspiration from the smog the architect noticed on the plane coming in. More beige, actually, than brown.

I had flown in through the same smog for the opening of a film I had made, past the same cylindrical building into a hotel room with the same cylindrical trash can. Everything was in those hungover shades of beige. The film was a remake of a Jean-Pierre Melville gem that I had called *The Good Thief* and it starred the great Nick Nolte. It had played in the Toronto festival, to a good reception, but Nick had been arrested driving on the Pacific Coast Highway under the influence of exhaustion from his press tour. The problem was that

Nick had played a heroin addict in *The Good Thief* and had told the press he had experimented with 'tar' while preparing for the part. So they claimed he was under the influence of something other than exhaustion and his mugshot was on every news-stand across these United States. I hoped the days when any publicity is good publicity were not entirely over. But I suspected they might be.

Anyway, I was driving in my hired car out towards Santa Monica to walk, when I noticed the Nuart, on my way there. I always took Santa Monica Boulevard, could have got there much quicker on the 401, but I like my destination sharing the same name as my route there. I saw the marquee sign – *The Earrings of Madame de*, by Max Ophüls. I reached the exterior of Danny's Chop Suey, which always reminded me of the opening of a *Touch Of Evil*, parked in the car park opposite and could finally walk. Down the boardwalk to Muscle Beach where the impossible bodies did impossible things with weights and pull up bars, back past the best bookshop I've ever found, Small World Books, where I picked up the *LA Weekly* and saw that I could make the mid-afternoon screening. I drove back to the Nuart, parked again and crossed the street to the cinema.

There were six or eight people inside the auditorium. There was nothing hip or cool about this audience. But then Ophüls doesn't have the cult cachet of Sergio Leone, Dario Argento or Mario Bava. Mainly older men, as I remember, which was odd, given that in its day it could have been considered one of the quintessential 'women's films'. I won't describe the film here, apart from admitting it was and is extraordinary, with its tale of a pair of earrings passed from wife to jeweller to husband to lover travelling across the Mediterranean and back, to resolve its journey in a duel. Black and white, unlike *Lola Montès* with its riot of Technicolor, which was the only other Ophüls film I had seen in a cinema.

Maybe the other six or seven attendees were film critics, or academics, or wanderers in the vague circus like myself. I hung around the foyer afterwards to see would I recognize anyone, but didn't, so I crossed the boulevard to the tiny car park and found my car blessedly un-ticketed and intact. I drove home then for another night in the hotel room.

It was always the Sunset Marquis for me, with its rabbits bouncing around the back pool, where you could take a short walk up Alta Loma onto Sunset Boulevard, turn right and find yourself among the shelves of Book Soup, or, if you crossed the road, among the videos of Tower Records.

I wondered should I call Nick, but didn't. That would involve another drive, out to Malibu where he lived with his son Brawley and a conversation about whatever health supplements he was on at the time. Instead I tried to remember other Ophüls movies I had seen. I had a vague memory of *La Ronde*, and its round of affection (or syphilis) passing from one lover to another. That one I had seen on television. I had seen the reconstituted *Lola Montès* in all of its blazing cinemascope colour in a cinema in London.

And there was another, made in Hollywood with all of the sumptuous overstated décor with which Hollywood treated Europe (and their Europe always seemed to be in Vienna), *Letter from an Unknown Woman*. They all involved a round of transfers, of one item, (earrings) or emotion (love) or even person (Lola Montez herself) from one to another. *Letter from an Unknown Woman* was different, yet somehow the same. The transfer here was of a girl to a young model, to a married woman, all of whom encountered the same pianist. During each encounter, he assumes that he is meeting a different person. There is a seduction and a pregnancy and a letter of revelation, written from a poorhouse, and of course a duel.

I had seen it on late-night television, probably in Victoria Road, Marino, Dublin which was a long way from Santa Monica Boulevard. To say I remembered it in its entirety would be wrong. Various images – a young girl on the stairs of a provincial house, listening to a pianist lodger her parents have taken on, a café orchestra longing for a couple to stop dancing and go home, scenes on trains, real and imaginary. Generally, a sense of heart-breaking lost possibilities. But I had never forgotten the story. A series of meetings, each one of them misconstrued, one can't forget, the other can't remember.

I wandered up to Tower Records and found a copy. You could do that then. It showed Louis Jourdan and Joan Fontaine in one of those kisses that are physically impossible but beautiful to look at, particularly in black and white, with both of their lips perfectly displayed to the lens. Those mouths are never going to meet in any liveable reality. I watched it again back in the bungalow in the Sunset Marquis and saw one of those pictures 'they don't make anymore'. The problem was, I could see why. It stated its purpose at the start, and headed towards the inevitable tragic conclusion. But. She was even more disappointed by her loved one's abuse of his talent than by his lack of recognition. And his servant was a mute. There was knowingness everywhere. It just seemed to have bypassed the central characters.

It was odd, this feeling of a story that haunts and you don't know why. You want it to explain itself, or go away.

One way to make it go away would be to remake it. But I had just done that with *Bob le flambeur* and Nick Nolte. And, by the way, how was that going? It had just been 'platformed' (they did that then) in about a hundred cinemas and received good, sometimes ecstatic notices. But there was the problem of the mugshot of Nick. I met him some days later and we did the Larry King show together, but none of the talk was about the movie, all of the talk was about addiction and recovery. So, Neil, tell me about your addictions. I'm addicted to stories, Larry.

I had invented a double heist for that one, which to me solved the nagging problem of a remake. One of the heists was faithful to the original. But everyone wants to rob a casino. Not everyone wants to be misremembered for a lifetime.

I met Peter Rice, the handsome and unusually sympatico president of Searchlight Pictures. So, Peter, you're probably going to let it play out in those hundred or so cinemas and then let it fade away? To my amazement he told the truth. He said yes.

I flew home, but the black and white movie, and more particularly, the story stuck with me. Almost like an earworm, the way certain pieces of popular music take residence in your brain and won't go away. They have an immediate familiarity, they seem to have always been there, they become part of your internal landscape. And you wish they would go away. But they won't.

A few years later I got my hands on the novel, by Stefan Zweig. The hero was a writer here, and so it lost two things. Writers aren't glamorous and have to be explained. Music never has to be explained. It had none of the swoon of the Ophüls film, which made me realize what a genius Ophüls was. That heightened sense of irony, even of artificiality, seemed to have vanished entirely. In fact, I realized, the humour that *The Grand Budapest Hotel* claimed to find in Zweig is non-existent in Zweig himself, as is the dark field of irony that Kubrick tried to put into *Eyes Wide Shut*, itself based on a Zweig story. What is there is a kind of delirious melodrama. An almost Victorian melodrama, heightened by the sense of a European culture of extremes, almost about to blow itself apart.

I was about to forget it again when I remembered the Father Mathew Hall.

The Father Mathew Hall was an out-of-the-way concert or function hall, on the Northside of inner city Dublin. On the extension of Drumcondra Road, actually, although I always remembered it as on the North Circular. I used to play the classical guitar as a young teenager, and was bludgeoned by my teacher into competing at the Father Mathew Feis Ceoil. He thought I was a musical genius. The judges – various luminaries from the College of Music, and Trinity College, plus one visiting celebrity – didn't. I don't remember who the celebrity was – it wasn't Julian Bream or John Williams, who would have been gods to any guitar-playing kid – probably a pianist in vogue at the time. But I remember my sweating hands as I worked my way through whatever piece of the repertoire I had chosen – probably Bach – and the dazzling proficiency of the one who followed me, who won the prize. I was given a special mention, or recommendation – some kind of embossed document – and resolved never to compete again.

What if, I thought, an aspiring pianist had to play before her hero, and was condemned to remember a series of encounters that he didn't?

What if she herself changed, and he didn't? We all have to change, go through various fashions, from Bowie glitter to New Romantic, to punk and on to various modes I'm too old to have the terms for. Nobody sticks in the decorous mittle-European style of Joan Fontaine in Hollywood's version of Vienna. Except maybe a concert pianist. The version of me that walked into the Nuart looked nothing like the kid who played his Bach preludes in the Father Mathew Hall.

So it still wouldn't go away. It was like a virus. And maybe stories are like viruses, they hang around in the borders of your consciousness, waiting for you to find the cure. And I had another virus to deal with.

The Astor was a small cinema on Eden Quay in Dublin. Nothing like the Nuart, it was a former concert hall that always seemed about to fall into the Liffey. Once called the Corinthian, but in 1967, like the Nuart, it showed the art movies everyone has forgotten about now. *Helga*, the sex education movie, played there, as did *Onibaba*, *Rashomon* and probably *Summer with Monika*, the kinds of movies that made you feel adult and eroticized at the same time. One of them was called *Lost Sex*, by the Japanese director who made *Onibaba*, Kaneto Shindo.

I can't remember much about *Onibaba*, something about a well and a field and samurai soldiers and murderous widows, but for some reason I remember the entire story of *Lost Sex*.

A kabuki actor (who could have played one of the samurais in *Onibaba*) has been suffering from the atomic fallout from Nagasaki (he can't have sex anymore) takes a house in a small Japanese hillside village. He is suffering from a crisis, both aesthetic (can't perform) and physical (can't perform). There are various scenes, awkward and almost risible, where he observes young lovers enjoying themselves in rural idylls. He hires a housekeeper, who tells him of a village custom, on their version of the week of Halloween, where the young men can mask themselves and visit the bedroom of the woman they desire.

The kabuki actor masks himself, crawls into her bedroom at night, and finds his affliction vanished. He can make love to her. But at the moment of passion, she mentions someone else's name. His subsequent jealousy destroys their burgeoning relationship, and he returns to Tokyo, to the theatre. But many years later, he returns to the village to find she has died. He asks, at her graveside, about the village custom. He is told there is no such thing, and realizes she made it all up.

It has the simplicity, even the naivety, of a folk tale, I suppose. Almost an allegory, from whatever lesson you choose can be drawn. Not too dissimilar to the story of the Ophüls movie. What they both had in common as well, was that there was other work, by both directors, that was better.

I happened to be in Tokyo, some years later again, as chairperson of the jury of the Tokyo Film Festival. I met Kaneto Shindo when they showed his latest (and last) movie, *Postcard*. It was quite beautiful and sad to see this film, in a Japanese culture where manga seems to be the prevailing aesthetic. I had to present an award to the gentleman, who was in his late nineties, and mentioned the story that I remembered from all those years ago. But the title was probably changed, for its European and definitely its Irish distribution. *Lost Sex* might at least draw in an audience, in Dublin in 1967. I'm not sure he understood me. And again, it wasn't his best. He didn't seem to remember, but nodded in that Japanese or old person way, as if to agree with everything.

Maybe he had forgotten it entirely. Maybe the exquisitely balanced house of cards we had inhabited was collapsing anyway. Maybe it had already collapsed. The Astor had long gone, Tower Records was gone, the rabbits were probably all dead around the Sunset Marquis pool.

So, I thought, maybe now I could forget about the story. But I couldn't. Someone inventing a legend, to make someone love them. It had the same power as the Zweig story. Someone meeting three times, and forgetting all about them.

By now I was well beyond sixty, and I was hit by an actual virus. I consider myself lucky. Some people get heart problems, some people get cancer. What I got was a severe skin affliction, a virulent form of psoriasis that turned my hands into something like the claws of a Komodo dragon. I could hardly type, let alone play the cello suites on the guitar, or show tunes on the piano. Everywhere I went, people offered me cures. Diets, vitamin extracts, salves that were based on goat's milk farmed in the Urals. My hands looked and felt like two lumps of stale, decaying bread, but they gave me an idea.

A pianist, whose hands are crippled by arthritic psoriasis, retires to a West Cork village where someone he never remembers lives.

There would have to be a well, not unlike the murderous pit in *Onibaba*.

I could begin with a sentence.

'He had met her three times and three times forgotten all about her.'

So it seemed to be a novel. Maybe the film would come later.

And maybe my hands would heal, with the typing.

Ghosts

I was still typing in the dream where I met Graham Greene. Like Ralph Fiennes in the film I had made of *The End of the Affair*, hammering out that immortal first line: 'This is a diary of hate.' He had heard I had made a film of his book and I apologized, said I should have asked his permission but, being dead, that might have been difficult. I could arrange a viewing for him. Or just give him a DVD. Or arrange a URL link, or whatever transmission system went from this world to the next.

I forget what period the dream was set in. He was definitely a figure from the fifties, dressed in mottled browny-green tweed, very tall, of the generation that drank gin and tonic with their lunch

Was this another father I had to please? An English one this time, with that clipped, Oxbridge way of talking. Could grammar be even more intimidating than mathematics? Everything an understatement, every sentence finished, no verb without its subject, object and modifier.

Maybe every film was an attempt to impress a father who didn't exist. Although in Greene's case, this would be blasphemous. God haunted him, there or not.

He met me two dream days later and expressed his confusion.

With the ending, I asked him, because I had changed his procession of miracles that made up the last twenty pages of the book?

I had retained one of them, a birthmark on a non-believer, and placed it on the cheek of the young son, of the detective, Parkis.

No, he said. With the whole thing. It seemed like marionettes moving on a stage set.

I am sorry.

Not your fault, he said. It's mine. I wrote them that way. You just made me realize it.

It was raining, in the second dream. I walked down a street in Mayfair, with a gaberdine coat over my head, entered a small restaurant and there he was.

It was the one where Bendrix realizes he has irretrievably fallen for Sarah. Ralph Fiennes reaches across the table and takes her hand.

He says, I'm in love, you know.

She says, me too.

Graham poured himself some wine. Greenish-tinged, into a fluted glass. He left mine empty.

And by the way, he asked, why so much rain?

Didn't you like the rain?

Only when he kissed her, on the street outside, both of them underneath his gaberdine coat. I remember that feeling.

The rain, I told him, helped me with the sense of unreality. It created a diffusion between the camera and the characters. The sense there was some other perspective, observing.

And besides, you wrote the opening in the rain.

My fault again.

And at last he poured me some wine. The wine tasted sour, like the past, like the conversation. But I liked him. I wondered if this was what being dead was like. Revisiting old loves, endlessly. There could be worse conditions.

Did you like the bomb?

The bomb was good. But then it led to the God thing.

It kind of had to.

The minute you introduce the God thing, you deprive the characters of agency.

You spent your whole life on what you call the God thing.

I know, he said. Is that why I've hated every adaptation of my work?

Even *The Third Man*?

He didn't answer. He lit a cigarette. You could smoke in this restaurant. So it must have been the fifties.

How do you shoot what isn't there?

What a realization, I thought. After a lifetime of questioning.

Yesterday upon the stair
I met a man who wasn't there.

He finished the quote for me. His memory was better than mine.

He wasn't there again today,
Oh how I wish he'd go away!

John Calley, who had come to rescue Columbia from the doldrums, was as obsessed with the novel as I was. He had asked me to adapt it for several years, and I put it off for years, making a gambling movie called *The Good Thief* and a horror film called *In Dreams*. Eventually he said, stop messing around and just do it. So I did it.

For some reason I remember the writing more than the shooting. It was possible to reduce it to very simple elements. A set of encounters, sexual, of course, remembered in different ways by different people. A bomb that hits a bedroom, where one character dies. The other prays him back to life. An overwhelming jealousy then on the part of the narrator, of an imagined lover who turns out not to exist.

I had a problem with the ending, as did Greene himself. He was a believer of a sort, the kind of Catholic convert who relished his own struggles with belief. I wasn't a Catholic convert, in fact an unbeliever who had grown up with this irrationality, but still retained a fascination for it. As James Joyce said, when asked why he didn't become a Protestant, why exchange a rational absurdity for an irrational one? So I found the logic of Greene's set of beliefs fascinating but felt, as many others did, that the last chapters dived into a series of irrationalities, in other words, miracles, that would be impossible to dramatize, even if they did exist. So I changed things towards the end, which may be what my dream was about.

Forgive me, Graham.

The most difficult part to cast was that of the cuckolded husband. When Bendriz, the lover, tries to silence the sounds of her orgasm in case her husband hears, she tells him not to worry, because he wouldn't know what the sound was. Who wants to play such a figure? I asked Stephen Rea to consider the role. He was offended, initially, but came to see that this other, patient and rejected lover could be as interesting a part as the novelist lover himself. Ralph Fiennes played the novelist, with a bitter intensity. Stephen gave a performance in the end that I found moving in its restraint, and the lost situation in which both widowed lovers find themselves was as plaintive as the love story itself. Who loves whom, most completely, in the end? It is hard to say. But Greene's conclusion, in the book, with both men inhabiting the house and remembering the absent Sarah, was the same as in the film.

Throughout the shooting, Catherine Walston's son, Oliver, turned up, dressed in a belted Norfolk jacket, anxious to witness the dramatization of his mother's affair with his father's rival. A situation I found as odd as the one portrayed at the end of the film. We discussed their affection, which led them from his father's estate to a cottage in Achill, exercised sometimes in brothels and sometimes behind high altars in Italy. The passion, the transgression, the heartache. Was his father as complaisant as Henry? His sense was that Greene never fully recovered from it. But Julianne Moore, he told me, brought his mother back to life.

I showed the film to John Calley in the Columbia screening room. When the lights came up, he was nowhere to be seen. I went up to the projection room and found him on the metal stairs outside, in tears. It reminded him of some distant, long-dead affection. He tried to explain it, but it wasn't necessary. I understood the feeling, too well, myself.

Later, I'm at the Golden Globes where we've been nominated in several categories. Julianne Moore for best actress, me for best director and Roger Pratt for best cinematography. I'm on the plane home, wondering if this, of all the films I made, might have satisfied my father. I probably found the book first on his shelves beside the fireplace. He would often buy two copies of books, forgetting he had already bought the first. Remembering the arguments at the red-lozenged kitchen table, the copybooks dragged from my hands, the rejections from publishers opened in my absence. The first reviews on the book programmes, in the *Irish Independent*, the *Irish Times*. Writing seemed to terrify him, maybe because it could reveal so much. If you let your ideas run riot, where would they end up? Probably some distance from the Dollymount seafront, swinging an umbrella on your daily constitutional.

Movies might have held less terror, ironically, because to both of us they were always full of terror. He would have enjoyed the vampires, ghosts and werewolves. But it was imagined terror. The humming of the power lines in Fairview Park on the walk back from the Fairview Cinema, an exact echo of the sound of bat's wings in Terence Fisher's *Dracula*. The crumbling façade of the crescent across from the park where Bram Stoker lived. All of them promised a haunting that never happened.

Ralph Fiennes as Bendrix wrestles with a God he doesn't believe in. He hates this jealous lover and his very hatred brings this absence into existence. Maybe it's a paradox my father would have appreciated.

My mother did.

I remembered standing by his grave. A flattened stone: no one on this rainy hillside below Howth Head was afforded the dignity of a plinth. Maybe it was some council order, to retain the symmetry of this field of the dead, as it curved away towards Howth Summit. I felt what Bendrix must have felt, saying come on, haunt me, Father, touch my arm some night and leave it withered, prove you still exist.

But all he left was a silence.

She never married again. Multiple suitors came calling. Pipe-smoking baritones or basses from her dead husband's choir. I encouraged her to remarry. She was still beautiful, active, engaging. But I could never work out why the thought didn't appeal to her. She had five sisters to spend time with. A caravan in Bettystown in which to park them all each summer. I didn't buy them a house, I bought them a caravan. On Lynch's Caravan Site, across from the eighteenth hole of the golf course, a mile or two from the post office in Mornington where she had been born. When her own health began to fail, and trips to those Portakabins that ringed the car park in Beaumont Hospital became more and more frequent, I often wondered did she wish she had. Married again. But maybe one romance is enough for a lifetime. Maybe it proved too tough for her, soured her on the possibility of another. Or maybe it was altogether too sweet, the dead become sweeter than the living.

Because the father has a presence like a sharp blade; I can hear the click of those heels, the scrape of the umbrella, each fragment of memory is like sand in a summer sandwich, crunches into being, demands its moment. The mother blends into the sea, the clouds, the mist round the sycamores in St Anne's Estate. One is a series of memories, the other becomes memory.

I was sitting beside a nun, of all beings, in the first-class cabin and a ferocious hammering of turbulence began. The nun, elderly, but with the kind of bloodless, unlined skin that nuns seem to specialize in, was particularly terrified. My seat was paid for by Columbia Pictures, and I had no idea who paid for hers. Maybe the Little Sisters of the Poor. Whatever order she belonged to, it gave her no reassurance. She grabbed my arm as the plane dropped another two hundred or so feet, sending all the baggage skittering. I took her hand, tried to calm her down. It will be OK, I told her, only a few air pockets, nothing to worry about. Come on, I thought to myself, you're a nun, you believe in this imaginary afterlife, the situation should be what Fluther Good called Vice Versa, you should be reassuring me. And I closed my eyes, as the plane did another whoomp, and when I opened them, there he was.

Standing, framed by the cone of the cockpit. Dressed in the cardigan with the leather patches that my mother had probably sewed on the elbows, hands in the woolly pockets. My mother, who was still alive, and awaiting my visit back to Dublin. The glasses still perched on the bridge of his nose, the eyes looking not at me but downwards, into mid-air, as if he was still trying to formulate a particularly elusive mathematical equation. One of those I always failed at.

Come on, Father, I remember thinking, ghosts don't appear in planes, tumbling through the air at 35,000 feet. Ghosts appear in Rosses Point, in Elphin, Roscommon, in the flattened graveyard you were buried in. Not in the first-class cabin of a 747. But he was there, without a doubt, and maybe the abstraction of his gaze was an attempt to work out his current condition. It must be difficult, and perplexing, being dead. Just ask Graham Greene.

I turned to the nun, and squeezed her arm, told her it would calm down soon, it would all be OK.

And maybe it was.

Acknowledgements

Thanks to: everyone who's mentioned in these pages. Forgive me if I've got anything wrong.

To: my children, Sarah, Anna, Ben, Daniel, Dashiel.

My wife, Brenda. (Read it now...)

To: Neil Belton and the team at Head of Zeus.

About the Author

NEIL JORDAN is an Irish film director, screenwriter and author based in Dublin. His first book, *Night in Tunisia*, won a Somerset Maugham Award and the *Guardian* Fiction Prize in 1979. He is also a former winner of the Rooney Prize for Irish Literature, the Irish PEN Award and the Kerry Group Irish Fiction Award. Jordan's films include *Angel*, the Academy Award-winning *The Crying Game*, *Michael Collins*, *The Butcher Boy* and *Interview with the Vampire*.

Image Credits